D1234866

How to Sell and Market Industrial Products

How to Sell and Market Industrial Products

By Wilbert H. Steinkamp

Chilton Book Company PHILADELPHIA NEW YORK LONDON

Foreword

To those who have the basic personality qualifications, plus motivation and drive, sales offers a challenging and rewarding career—one which frequently leads to upper management job opportunities.

This book was written for the salesman and his supervisors and for the home office marketing staff. It can serve as a refresher for the experienced salesman, and it will be invaluable for the beginner and for those who are thinking about entering the sales engineering profession. All of the subject matter is applicable to the home office marketing organization, and the material can be used as a guide upon which specific, product-oriented training programs can be built.

The text offers practical, analytical, and logical sales methods which have proven by years of creative and competitive selling of technically oriented products in diversified industrial and government markets.

The book purports to develop the total salesman by including appropriate marketing and management development principles which he can use to his advantage.

The author realizes that training is not something which is done to the individual, but rather something which he must do for himself. Ninety per cent of all successful development results from application on the job and from self study and practice by the individual on his own. The text stresses this self-development philosophy and gives practical examples and illustrations of how the fundamentals should be applied. Specific recommendations are made at the end of several chapters covering homework and on-the-job practice assignments which are vital to acquiring the skills needed for most profitable application of the material.

Contents

Part 3 • Marketing and Management in the Sales Territory

Part 4 • The Home Office Marketing Function

Part 1
The Salesman

The Makeup of a Successful Salesman

Charles M. Schwab, of the steel industry, stated some years ago that, "We are all salesmen, every day of our lives. We are selling our ideas, our plans, our enthusiasm to those with whom we come in contact." This is certainly true with respect to interpersonal relationships during our daily lives. Many sales fundamentals are applied subconsciously in our social and business relationships. The concept that salesmen are born is true only to the extent that some of us are born with at least the potential to develop a few of the personality traits which make for success in selling. Much more than this is involved, of course, and the successful salesman is made rather than born to the profession. He is self-made to a large degree.

Selling is a challenging and rewarding profession; it is also a very demanding one. High on the list of qualifications is industriousness — the willingness to work hard and to put in long hours, sometimes in speculation of short-range rewards. Motivation, perseverence and drive are indispensable attributes for success. Successful selling combines both artistic and scientific talents, most of which can be acquired with training and self development.

The make-up of a successful sales engineer may be illustrated in the accompanying triangular configuration, with the personality

MAKEUP OF A SALES ENGINEER

qualifications occupying the apex segment, knowledge qualifications comprising the center segment, and salesmanship qualifications comprising the base segment.

The personality qualifications are perhaps the most important factor in the initial consideration of an applicant for a selling position. Some of the applicant's traits become apparent during the first interview. Others must be ascertained by psychological testing, reference checks, and additional in-depth interviews. The lack of certain traits can be a serious handicap from the beginning, and it may eventually be an important determining factor in the progress and the ultimate achievement of the individual.

Of the three qualifications illustrated in the triangle, personality is the most difficult to define, because personality is a composite of an individual's strengths and weaknesses. While there is no ideal personality specification, it is possible to single out certain traits which most successful salesmen have in common. The presence or lack of some of these can usually be learned before an applicant is employed. These early judgements can be confirmed by observing the individual during the initial phase of his training.

The applicant should be neat and well-groomed, and his manner should be warm and outgoing. He is one who enjoys being with people and who meets and gets acquainted with new people easily and comfortably.

The candidate must be industrious, willing to work late hours and have the energy to sustain such drive.

Persistence and a sense of humor are also very desirable attributes. In summary, it should be pointed out that a man's personality is the result of three primary influences: heredity, environment, and self development. Heredity is a significant factor which is uncontrollable. Environment, which forms lasting impressions and deep-rooted habits is most important. Self development speaks for itself as an ingredient of personality.

Unfortunately, the personality qualifications are the least amenable to change and improvement, and they are, therefore, the least controllable factor in stimulating and accelerating professional growth. This observation is made to emphasize by contrast the immediate and continuing improvement opportunities in the Knowledge and Salesmanship segments of our triangle.

The Knowledge segment is all-encompassing. It includes the basic technical education which the man brings with him as an applicant, and continuing home or post-graduate studies, relating to his daily work, which most successful sales engineers engage in. Quite often, such extra-curricular activities are offered by the employer on an optional, subsidized basis. The rapid advance in technology in virtually all industry makes it imperative for the salesman to keep abreast of progress so that he can better understand the needs of his customer when applying his products.

This segment also includes a thorough knowledge of his com-

4

pany's products and those of his principal competitors. Detailed knowledge of the application of these products and of the benefits to the customer must also be understood. Prices and company policies must be understood. In marketing, it includes knowledge of the customers and prospects and of the competitor's activities. Everything in this segment of the triangle can be acquired by study and effort.

To the new sales engineer, product knowledge is the most important requirement in order to get started in his career. As he acquires this proficiency in all facets of this knowledge group, he becomes

PREPARE FOR FUTURE GROWTH

more confident, more competent, and more effective. His major concern thereafter is to keep up with the new products and the new applications of his products. He is also concerned about changes in trends which affect the requirements for his products. The sales engineer usually tries to keep conversant with these changes by reading technical trade publications and by participating in the activities of appropriate technical societies.

Knowledge should continue to increase throughout the salesman's entire career, because it has a definite bearing on the degree of success which the sales engineer attains. Many have achieved modest success because of their knowledge and because they have a normal complement of personality traits. They service their customers efficiently and maintain satisfactory relationships between the customers and their company. There was a time when the term sales engineering connoted just this type of activity — engineering service for their customers. This interpretation is no longer valid or applicable.

Salesmanship is the most important ingredient to assure maximum earnings and consideration for advancement. Ours is a fast moving economy. Rapid technological advancement and the accompanying requirement for better performing machinery, apparatus, and instrumentation have stimulated the development of many new products. Such products must be sold creatively by discovering the need, offering a sound solution to satisfy the need, and, most important, by selling the economic advantages to the customer.

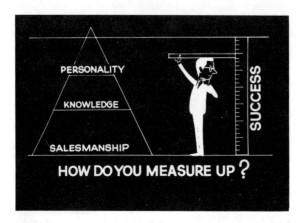

The salesman must have a thorough knowledge of the fundamentals of salesmanship and must develop the skills to apply these fundamentals to create and negotiate sales.

The Makeup of a Successful Sales Manager

All of the traits which are essential for the success of the sales engineer are equally important for the success of the sales supervisor. These include all of the personality traits plus demonstrated imagination and creativeness. Obviously, the sales supervisor must have considerable knowledge and proven salesmanship aptitudes and capabilities.

The surest way to win consideration for a supervisory job is by outstanding performance as a salesman. This does not happen quickly. It may take a minimum of several years and, more typically, five or more years in the field to acquire diversified experience and to demonstrate ability and readiness for advancement. The experience which the sales engineer acquires in analyzing his territory and planning his account coverage efficiently and productively can be an invaluable asset in a supervisory position.

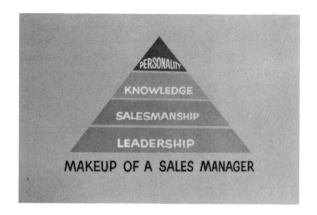

MAKEUP OF A SALES MANAGER

Our triangle now contains a fourth segment—leadership. Obviously the sales supervisor must be a good personal leader. He must be able to motivate new salesmen and to supervise and coach them effectively. He must learn how to review the performance of his men, including appraisal and counseling, on a regular basis. He must understand how to set goals and how to apply the necessary controls for the performance of salesmen. The supervisor must become skillful in recruiting and selecting new salesmen. Not all salesmen have the leadership qualities or motivations to advance to supervisor. Many top-notch salesmen make substantial incomes and are completely happy with the challenge of handling the large producing customers on a continuing basis. However, virtually all sales supervisors and sales managers rise from the sales level, and this experience and background are the most important requisites for such advancement.

The Selling Job — Typical Duties of a Sales Engineer

Sales engineering has been defined as the art of selling equipment and services which require engineering skill in their selection, application and use. It combines a knowledge of salesmanship plus specialized technical education and training in order to render a service to the customer. The following are representative duties of a typical sales engineer:

TYPICAL DUTIES OF A SALESMAN

1. Studying the products to be sold—literature, prices and operating instructions.
2. Analyzing the customer's specifications and requests for quotations.
3. Requesting information from the home office for the preparation of proposals and quotations.
4. Preparing the proposals and quotations and handling correspondence with prospects and customers.
5. Analyzing customers' complaints and correcting trouble with the equipment or its application.
6. Conferences with company associates, sales meetings, etc.
7. Making out reports, correcting mailing lists, assisting in the preparation of sales forecasts and territory analysis.
8. Traveling to and from customer offices and factories.
9. Representing the company at technical and customer-industry group meetings and exhibits.
10. Entertaining customers.
11. Creatively selling products and services.

From the foregoing, it is apparent that there are at least ten essential duties which, in effect, must compete for a share of the time which the salesman devotes to creatively selling the products and services of his company. Obviously, this is the most important duty of all. The salesman who is a good planner and a good manager of his time will usually rate high in percentage of face-to-face selling hours. He will also score high in quota accomplishment and earnings.

Self Development

Now that we have analyzed the make-up of a typical successful sales engineer and the criteria for success as a sales supervisor, we should consider ways of achieving these essential qualifications.

SELF DEVELOPMENT

All successful development is self development. Ninety per cent of all development progress is accomplished either by application on the job or in self study and practice by the individual on his own time. Knowledge without application is worthless.

Take a Look at Yourself

Whether you are a field sales engineer, a district manager, a regional manager, or a marketing manager, it is good practice to take an objective look at yourself periodically and to try to appraise your strengths and weaknesses in your present capacity as well as in relation to other positions in sales or marketing to which you may aspire. To analyze oneself objectively is difficult. Sometimes the goals or standards that provide a basis for comparison are not clearly defined. Some attempt will be made now to provide a basis for such comparisons — first with respect to the psychological traits which you

possess, and then with respect to how you utilize your most valuable asset—the time available for accomplishing your objectives.

Psychological Profile of the Star Salesman

Several years ago the Sales and Marketing Executives Association of Los Angeles conducted a study entitled the "Star Salesman." The author cooperated as a member of the club's research committee in planning and administering the study and the psychological firm— Aptitude Testing for Industry—cooperated in administering tests and assisting in summarizing the results. The objectives of this study were to help sales managers improve procedures used for selecting

salesmen and to determine whether star salesmen have behavior traits in common and whether these traits can be identified in advance of hiring. The results of this study have many other uses, the most important of which is to provide men, now engaged in selling, with a basis for comparing their own corresponding psychological traits. A total of sixty companies cooperated in this project by offering 97 men as examples of outstanding salesmen. These men were divided into four general product groups, and retail, door-to-door, and route salesmen were not included. The breakdown by product groups follows:

Product Group	Number of Salesmen
Technical sales	26
Industrial sales	39
Intangible sales	21
Consumer products at wholesale	11

Sixty-seven per cent of the men participating were selling industrial products.

The findings were compiled from data commonly used in hiring salesmen and comprised the following:

1. Personal background information concerning the nominee. This form, identified as Exhibit A, was filled out in detail by the star salesman suggested by the employer.
2. Employer's ratings—identification by the sales manager of the traits which in his judgement contributed most to the success of the salesman. This is identified as Exhibit B.
3. Comprehensive psychological tests covering mental ability, personality and motivation were administered by the psychological firm mentioned earlier. The results of these tests are shown on Charts I and II.

Some of the conclusions based on these three data sources follow:

1. Biographical and personal.
   A. He had previous, demonstrated, sales experience.
   B. He may have attended college, but except for the technical salesman, he probably didn't finish.
   C. In his spare time he is very active in sports, usually of a competitive sort.
2. Attitude toward selling.
   A. He chose selling as a career—he didn't drift into it.
   B. He knew it would be hard work but he expected to make more money.
   C. He would choose selling again if he were to start over.

SME STAR SALESMAN PROJECT — PERSONAL BACKGROUND INFORMATION

Exhibit A

Name_____

Address_____

Date_____

Phone_____

Occupational Preferences: ANSWER THE FOLLOWING QUESTIONS BY GIVING YOUR PREFERENCE AS THEY ARE TODAY. List below 4 occupations in which you would like to earn your living, if you could start over. Do not consider your age, abilities, experience or job opportunities. Consider only whether or not you would be happy in the work.

Occupation	Reason for Choice
1st Choice_____	
2nd Choice_____	
3rd Choice_____	
4th Choice_____	

Work Satisfaction: In each of the following pairs, check the one that you would prefer.

☐ PRACTICAL, SPECIFIC work that is well organized and planned.

or

☐ ABSTRACT, CREATIVE work that frequently changes, requiring independent action to work out unexpected problems.

☐ Work activities dealing with THINGS and OBJECTS.

or

☐ Work activities concerned with COMMUNICATING IDEAS and involving PEOPLE (not actually dealing with people in person).

☐ Work resulting in PRESTIGE and ESTEEM from other people.

or

☐ Work that is basically SELF-SATISFYING because of tangible, productive results.

☐ Work primarily SOCIAL in nature — related to personal dealings with people and working for their own good or betterment.

or

☐ Work primarily NONSOCIAL in nature — related to production, processes, machines and techniques.

☐ Work activities involving BUSINESS CONTACTS with PEOPLE.

or

☐ Work activities of a SCIENTIFIC and TECHNICAL nature.

☐ Work involving a wide VARIETY of tasks.

or

☐ Work concentrating on a FEW major tasks.

Circle TWO of your check marks to show which aspects of work are the MOST IMPORTANT to you.

GENERAL

Did you expect that selling would appreciably increase your income? Yes ☐ No ☐

Did you expect that selling would appreciably increase your working hours? Yes ☐ No ☐

How did you get into selling? ☐ Influence of family/friends. ☐ By choice. ☐ Best job available at the time. ☐ Pushed into it.

(over)

ANSWER THE FOLLOWING QUESTIONS AS OF THE DATE YOU WERE HIRED. GIVE ALL FACTS AS THEY WERE THEN.

Age_____ Height_____ Weight_____

Marital Status: Were you: Single ☐ Married ☐ Separated ☐ Divorced ☐ Widower ☐ Remarried ☐

With whom did you live?_____

Dependents: Including yourself, how many people did you support?_____

How many children did you have?_____ Ages?_____

Home Ownership: Did you rent? Yes ☐ No ☐ Check One: Apt. ☐ Home ☐ Room ☐

Did you own your home? Yes ☐ No ☐ Did you own your home clear? Yes ☐ No ☐

Income: Were you paying off a loan on your home? Yes ☐ No ☐ Amount/year $_____

Did you have any income other than your salary? Yes ☐ No ☐

Locality: Where did you live during most of your childhood? City ☐ Small town ☐ Rural ☐

Interests: What were your main hobbies or leisure time activities at the time of hiring?

Work history: Fill in your work experience for your last 6 jobs.

Title of Job	Months/Years on Job	Title of Job	Months/Years on Job
1.		4.	
2.		5.	
3.		6.	

Which of your last 6 jobs did you like the best?
Why?
Which of your last 6 jobs did you like the least?
Why?

SME STAR SALESMAN PROJECT — BEHAVIOR TRAITS LIST

Star Salesman's Name _____ Company Name _____ Sales Manager's Name _____

Please circle the number opposite the **5 traits** which contribute most of this Star Salesman, and check **the one** which you consider the primary source of this achievement. Example: V⟨14⟩ Loves money.

1. Sizes up people very well.
2. Mentally alert — thinks on his feet.
3. A very hard worker.
4. Competitive spirit — won't let anyone get ahead of him.
5. Flexible and adaptable — can shift strategy under emergency conditions.
6. Plans and organizes well.
7. Fundamentally runs scared.
8. Works primarily for benefit of family.
9. Is insecure — has to keep proving his adequacy.
10. Uses highly creative approach.
11. Loves to sell.
12. Can meet and handle people at all levels.
13. Sociable — never meets a stranger — loves people, people like him.
14. Loves money.
15. "Lives his job."
16. Cooperative — congenial with fellow workers.
17. Persuasive
18. Gets his prime satisfaction from servicing accounts.

19. Tactful.
20. Has sound practical judgment.
21. Inspires confidence.
22. Takes turndowns and disappointments in stride.
23. Stands on his own feet — handles accounts, makes decisions with minimum of help.
24. A plugger — won't give up.
25. Gives careful attention to detail.
26. Has interest in keeping up to date.
27. Has no hesitancy in asking for orders.
28. Always enthusiastic.
29. Wants to be top man.
30. Is serious-minded.
31. Not sensitive — can take criticism without making excuses.
32. Fast worker — speedy — always on the go.
33. Self-starter.
34. Has "nose for business."
35. Works smart — not just hard.
36. Responsible — can be counted on by customers and by us.

37. _____
(Other)

Nobody's perfect — If you could make him over, what would you change in him? _____

*** Use reverse for any additional comments. ***

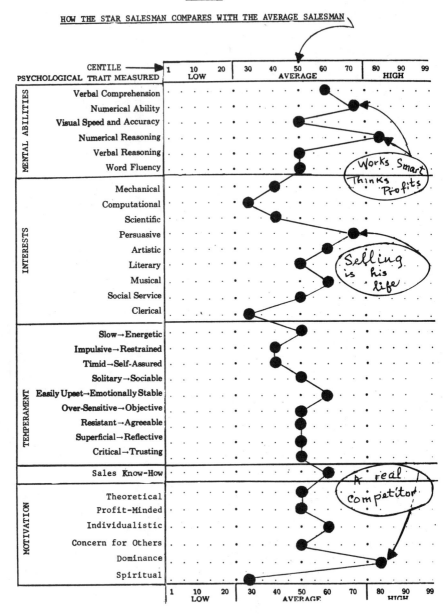

CHART I

HOW THE STAR SALESMAN COMPARES WITH THE AVERAGE SALESMAN

D. He likes his job because it's challenging and demanding.
3. As his boss sees him. He is successful because:
   A. He works smart—not just hard.
   B. He won't let anyone get ahead of him.
   C. He is very responsible, as well as a hard worker.
4. How he looks on tests (Charts I and II):
   A. He's brighter—especially in figuring and in working with profit and cost figures.
   B. He'd rather sell than eat.
   C. He wants his way and will struggle to get it.
   D. He is mature and emotionally stable.

WHAT THE STAR SALESMAN IS NOT LIKE

Some psychologists have advanced the view that a successful sales-man is a kind of psychological compensation case. One writer states that, "the salesman is a man who is characterized by the conviction that he is really unloved and unwanted and he must buy the affection of all with whom he comes into contact, using personal charm, flattery, gifts and similar inducements."

Another writer claims that the outstanding salesman is often an introvert and acts like an extrovert because he knows that by doing so makes him acceptable to the buyer. Some sales managers believe that the successful man is a tall man. Others think that single men chase women, not customers. These ideas are refuted by both sales managers' observations and psychological test data on the 97 sales-men included in this study. Instead, the star salesman emerges as a man who is superior in emotional stability, the ability to stand on his own feet, to take turn-downs and so on. Of 624 behavior traits listed, only three sales managers mentioned that the salesman "fundament-ally runs scared" and five stated that he is insecure and "has to keep proving his adequacy." No mention was made of introvert qualities as a success trait.

Emotional stability test scores reveal the star salesman to be better able than 60% of salesmen generally and 85% of the general popula-tion to maintain his morale. Similarly, in sociability he exceeds 85% of the general population and 50% of the average salesmen generally.

Finally, his height is average for southern California, which is 5'11". The star salesmen range from 5'5" to 6'4" tall. Thus, the star salesman is evidently no psychological oddball but rather a person much better able than most to stand the strains of life, as well as the special strains of being a salesman.

How is the Star Salesman Different?

The evidence derived from sales managers' ratings, personal history data and psychological tests is that the star salesman differs far more from the general population in ways that can be determined in advance of hiring, than he does from the average salesman. However, the star salesman does differ from his fellow salesmen in the following respects:

1. Superior mental abilities. Sales managers' observations of mental alertness were confirmed by mental ability tests, the results of which indicate that the average star salesman surpasses:

   80% of salesmen generally and 90% of the general population in numerical reasoning;
   70% of salesmen generally and 80% of the general population in numerical ability;
   60% of salesmen generally and 90% of the general population in verbal comprehension;
   50% of salesmen generally and 80% of the general population in verbal reasoning;
   50% of salesmen generally and 80% of the general population in visual speed and accuracy;
   50% of the salesmen generally and 70% of the general population in word fluency.

Only nine salesmen had intelligence ratings significantly below average (for salesmen) and of these only four failed to meet minimum intelligence standards usually applied to sales applicants.

The conclusion was that mental ability tests are an essential tool for identifying men capable of becoming star salesmen. Further, such tests will eliminate at least 90% of men incapable of becoming top producers. Such tests are readily available, inexpensive and simple to use.

2. Greater competitive spirit. Drive is more difficult than intelligence to determine in advance of hiring. The sales manager must imaginatively inquire into present and past behavior which reflect the candidate's urge to win. Specific study findings:

   A. Active participation in sports. Over 60% of the star salesmen listed sports or airplane piloting as their chief hobby.
   B. Dominance on test data. The star salesman exceeds 80% of the salesmen generally in dominance — defined as the urge to win out in face-to-face dealings and generally to get his way. In closely allied factors of flexibility and resourceful-

CHART II

HOW THE STAR SALESMAN COMPARES WITH THE AVERAGE MAN

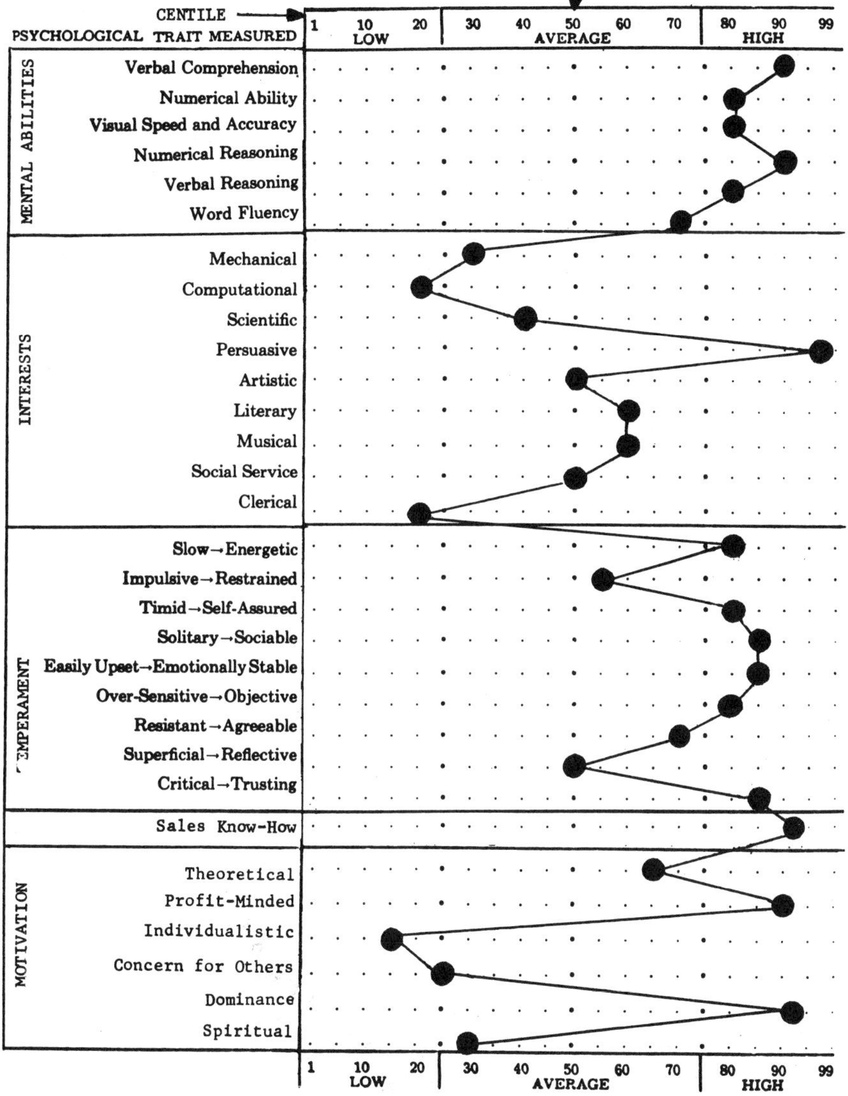

	CENTILE →	1	10 LOW	20	30	40	50 AVERAGE	60	70	80	90 HIGH	99
PSYCHOLOGICAL TRAIT MEASURED

MENTAL ABILITIES
- Verbal Comprehension
- Numerical Ability
- Visual Speed and Accuracy
- Numerical Reasoning
- Verbal Reasoning
- Word Fluency

INTERESTS
- Mechanical
- Computational
- Scientific
- Persuasive
- Artistic
- Literary
- Musical
- Social Service
- Clerical

TEMPERAMENT
- Slow→Energetic
- Impulsive→Restrained
- Timid→Self-Assured
- Solitary→Sociable
- Easily Upset→Emotionally Stable
- Over-Sensitive→Objective
- Resistant→Agreeable
- Superficial→Reflective
- Critical→Trusting

Sales Know-How

MOTIVATION
- Theoretical
- Profit-Minded
- Individualistic
- Concern for Others
- Dominance
- Spiritual

| | 1 | 10 LOW | 20 | 30 | 40 | 50 AVERAGE | 60 | 70 | 80 | 90 HIGH | 99 |

ness the star salesman exceeds nearly 70% of his fellow salesmen.

The conclusion from this is that every facet of a salesman's record indicative of competitiveness should be explored. Any form of struggle is a plus, but socially oriented competition like sports is probably preferable. A candidate's record, personal life and psychological make-up all provide clues to identifying the potential star salesman.

PREFERENCE FOR SELLING

Sales managers' ratings, test results and star salesmen themselves all agree that a liking for selling is a key success trait. Sales managers ranked it fourth among 36 traits accounting for the star's success.

The conclusion is that interviews should focus on why the candidate wants to get into selling. Personal history forms, if properly designed, can give clues as to actual interest. In addition, psychological tests appear helpful in determining whether the applicant really prefers selling over other activities.

These are the most significant findings from this star salesman project. They have been included here because they can be helpful to the salesman personally in providing a basis for comparison with his own traits. They can be helpful to the supervisor and the sales manager by providing certain standards and testing recommendations in the selection of new sales personnel.

How a Salesman Selling to Industry Spends his Time

The average salesman has approximately 220 days per year available to him for productive selling and the related essential supporting local office chores. This is arrived at as follows:

Total year = 52 weeks × 5 =		260 days
Deductions: holidays		10
	vacation	10
	home office meetings, training and trade show participation	15
	illness, moving and miscellaneous	5
	Total deductions	40
Total year		260
	Minus deductions	− 40
Net potential working days		220

Many studies have been made of the way the average salesman spends his time during these potential working days available to him. Typical of these is one conducted by the research division of the McGraw-Hill Company, which was issued during 1964. It is the summary report of questionnaires received from over a thousand industrial salesmen representing 193 industrial companies. The questionnaires related to their time utilization during a typical period during 1963.

The salesmen represented 12 industry categories and the allocation of their time was reported accordingly. The average industrial salesman, based on all 12 industry categories, put in an average work day of 9 hours and 22 minutes. Of this day, he was able to spend only 3 hours and 52 minutes in face-to-face selling. Traveling and waiting for interviews and paper work consumed slightly over half of his day. This is how the average industrial salesman's time was spent:

Reports, paper work, local sales meetings	20%
Service calls	5%
Traveling and waiting for interviews	34%
Face-to-face selling	41%

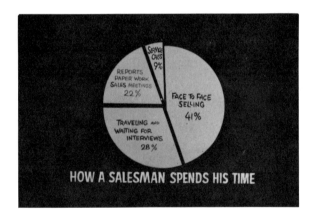

HOW A SALESMAN SPENDS HIS TIME

When you consider that this 41 percent of time spent in face-to-face selling applies only to the number of the potential selling days in the year this figure becomes more significant. Of the theoretical 52 weeks, or 260 work days, available per year, less than 220 productive working days remain. Forty-one percent of the 220 productive days would amount to 90 days which the average industrial salesman spends in face-to-face selling during a full year. It should be interesting to compare your own performance with these averages.

There were some other interesting sidelights of this study. The average salesman reporting was responsible for 111 active accounts and 103 prospect accounts, totaling 214 companies to be called on. They estimated there were four men in each company who recommend, specify, approve, or otherwise influence purchase of their products in the average company called on. This would make a total of 856 possible people to be contacted.

In the one day for which they kept diaries, the salesmen made 8.4 calls. This gave them an average of 28 minutes per individual. While this study is extremely interesting, it may or may not be truly representative of a salesman engaged in industrial selling, which involves highly specialized and sophisticated products and rather select and readily identifiable markets. These figures, therefore, cannot be considered as representative. Their principal value is to provide a comparison against which to check how you spend your own time. It should be obvious that there is a definite relationship between the percentage of face-to-face selling time and earnings. The salesman who becomes a good manager of his time has one important qualification for a bigger opportunity in selling and marketing management.

This subject will be discussed further in Part III under the heading: "Sales Territory Analysis, Customer Evaluation and Sales Coverage Planning."

Suggested Self-Development Exercises

In keeping with the self-development philosophy, it is appropriate to suggest some homework exercises relating to the subject matter which has been covered so far. Take a hard look at yourself, and try to make a frank assessment of your relative strengths in the three broad qualification categories.

In the personality category, make up a chart portraying yourself, similar to Chart I. In the left-hand column, list the traits grouped alongside the headings covering Mental Abilities, Interests, Temperament, and Motivation. Then list the percentage headings in vertical columns. Study the traits one by one and then try to estimate your own strength or weakness relative to the fiftieth percentile column which typifies the average salesman. This may seem like a meaningless or impractical task, but it is sure to be a beneficial one. The very act of thinking about yourself in terms of these predominant traits is bound to have some beneficial result, regardless of the accuracy of your self-assessment.

For men who may be contemplating going into the selling profession, it would be better to study Chart II and attempt to assess themselves in comparison with the average man. Virtually all of the traits registered above the fiftieth percentile are essential to success and happiness in the selling profession. If there are serious doubts about your ability to measure up to a majority of these essential traits, it would be a worthwhile investment to subject yourself to a few pertinent psychological tests. Some personality weaknesses which have to do with human relationships can be corrected by participation in courses which are designed for this purpose.

In the knowledge category, there is some room for self-assessment also. Ask yourself these questions:

1. Am I fully conversant with all of my company's products?
2. How familiar am I with my competitors' products?
3. With respect to the application and use of my products, have I made sufficient effort to keep abreast of the changes that are taking place in the industries with which I am concerned?
4. Do I periodically check up on changes that take place in my territory, e.g., customer personnel changes, new companies moving in, and new plant construction and expansion?
5. Am I doing any reading or taking evening classes to broaden my knowledge of marketing subjects?

In the salesmanship category, the very fact that you are reading this book is evidence that you desire to advance in your profession. Later, after you have studied the text carefully, you will be in a better position to appraise your selling habits and techniques. A worthy project to undertake now, and periodically in the future, is to make an analysis of your use of time for customer visits.

Utilizing a simple diary which lists the hours of each day, draw vertical columns headed:

1. Traveling and waiting for interviews
2. Reports, paper work, sales meetings
3. Service calls
4. Face-to-face selling

Place the appropriate number opposite the horizontal hourly figures and then, at the end of the day, summarize the hours devoted to each category. See how your percentages compare with the study previously referred to in the text. This is only one of many ways in which you may analyze your work habits to insure most efficient coverage of your territory.

Part 2
Salesmanship

The Steps to a Creative Sale

Whenever a truly creative sale is made, six distinct steps or phases are accomplished. Breaking the sale into such elementary steps may seem only theoretical, but such analysis and definition is extremely important to the salesman. He must understand these steps and become familiar with their normal sequence. He must be conscious

of them on every sales call so that he can appraise his progress toward making the sale. The salesman does not necessarily follow each of these steps in every sales situation. But they are always accomplished by one means or another. Some of them may be taken in advance of the salesman's call. For example, attention and interest may result from the efforts of the market research department, returns from direct mail advertising, inquiries from trade paper advertising, trade show activities and other home office promotional activities. The steps to a sale are as follows:

1. Pre-approach
2. Approach
3. Attention
4. Interest
5. Desire
6. Decision

25

This important step comprises the advance preparation and planning for the sales call. Thorough advance preparation is absolutely necessary, yet, some salesmen—old pros as well as beginners—some-

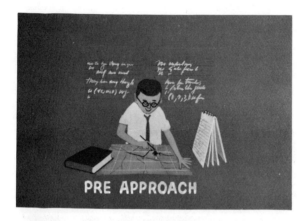

PRE APPROACH

times devote too little time, if any, to this important step. Successful salesmen make it a routine procedure to prepare and plan, in advance, for all sales calls. A checklist may be useful for this purpose.

Think of some of the common oversights based on your own experience.

1. Did I have a long wait in the reception room because I assumed my prospect could see me promptly, and, therefore, I did not make an appointment?
2. Did I neglect to check the route and, as a result, underestimated the travel time, thereby arriving at an inappropriate time to permit an interview?
3. Did I fail to bring the required literature, instructions, prices, drawings?
4. Did I check out the demonstrator or the visual presentation before I set it up in front of my prospect?
5. Did I check delivery, shipment shortage, overdue credit or whatever else I may have promised to do on the previous call?
6. Have I reviewed the files and possibly queried others to get the benefit of the history of my company's past relations with the prospect?
7. Have I established a goal for accomplishment on this call?

These are some of the typical pre-approach chores. Your list will probably include others which are pertinent to your particular business.

APPROACH

This is the manner in which the salesman meets his prospect. It includes his appearance, his smile, his opening statement or greeting, his hand shake and poise — plus any other outward factors that convey an impression of enthusiasm, sincerity and confidence. His introductory remarks are equally important. On an initial contact,

there are many things that the prospect needs to know about the salesman and his reason for being there before he can decide whether he should spend some time with him. The proper introduction will automatically put the prospect at ease, while a poorly phrased one may keep the prospect guessing.

In order to make an effective approach, the salesman must carefully watch his introduction, greeting, appearance, attitude, poise, and mood. A show of enthusiasm and a business-like manner will favorably impress any prospect.

The successful salesman also uses the approach to size up his prospect. There are many things he needs to know. He attempts to verify the prospect's mood at the time of the interview and then tries to adjust this mood so that the prospect is put in the right frame of mind for each succeeding step of the interview. During this interview, the salesman should also be conscious of the atmosphere or surrounding conditions under which the interview is being conducted and he should make an attempt to make these as favorable as possible. One typical example of this would be to suggest that the sales presentation or demonstration be conducted in a conference room instead of in a reception lobby or in the prospect's office where there may be many distracting influences. Here is a typical example of how a good salesman handles this kind of situation.

Salesman: "Good morning, Mr. Jones. My name is Jack Smith. I represent the ABC Instrument Company in this area. Your neighbor, Dick Brown, suggested that you might be interested to hear about a recent installation of ABC recorders in his new development laboratory. This new system is giving him a lot more data, in more readily usable form, and at a lower cost than any other system. I'd appreciate an opportunity to tell you more about it."

Customer: "That must be the new set-up that Dick mentioned at the Instrument Society meeting last week. We're not in the market for more recorders right now, but I'd like to hear about your new system."

Note that the salesman did three fundamental things to ensure getting an interview. First, he identified himself and his company clearly. Then he used the name of a mutual acquaintance to quickly gain acceptance. Finally, he referred in a general way to the benefits of the new recording system which was sold recently. This kind of approach is typical of several which may be used under similar circumstances.

ATTENTION

The objective is to get the prospect's undivided attention and, more important, his favorable attention, because favorable attention causes the prospect to believe, accept, and understand what the salesman is

going to tell him. The salesman cannot expect to arouse interest, let alone get an order, if the prospect's mind is full of doubts such as, "Is this fellow going to waste my time?" "Does he know his business?" "Can I trust him?" "Is he going to try and sell me something I don't need?" The salesman's introductory remarks should be directed at satisfactorily answering these questions.

28

The prospect is a busy man, and the salesman will have to compete for his attention against many other distracting influences. It is important, therefore, that the attention-getting technique be planned in advance. The salesman's opening remarks and the availability of some form of demonstration or other type of visual sales presentation can help to keep the prospect's attention. If the salesman fails to get the prospect's undivided attention, the call will be futile. The salesman should keep in mind that the average man receives more than 80 percent of his knowledge through his eyes. Impressions received by the eye are remembered longer than those that are heard. Furthermore, the average man remembers 10 percent of what he hears, but he remembers 30 percent of what he sees. He remembers 50 percent of what he both sees and hears. It is obvious that the sales engineer should always have some visual, attention-getting material with him on an initial sales call.

Here is an example of how the salesman can get his prospect's attention.

> *Salesman:* "That's fine, Mr. Jones, I brought along several things that will help explain this installation. I have some pictures, a schematic diagram, and a sample chart. Could we lay these out on the table somewhere? I have a recorder of this type in my car, and I will be glad to operate it for you after you look over the diagram and the test data."

The salesman could have given the customer a verbal description of this installation, referring to a catalog. The interview might have been continued and concluded while standing in the reception room. Obviously, this would not have been nearly as effective as the strategy which the salesman actually used. The mention of photographs, schematics, sample charts and an operating demonstration arouses the customer's curiosity and ensures getting his undivided attention in a favorable environment, away from distracting influences. The use of visual materials and demonstration products does more than command the customer's attention: it insures that he will remember more of what you tell him.

INTEREST

Interest must follow attention. If the salesman really has something to sell, he can easily advance to this step, but, to accomplish this, he must establish the relationship between the prospect or his company and the salesman's products or services. The prospect must know early in the interview how the products relate to his business. The salesman may accomplish this by pointing out, in broad terms, some of the benefits that could result from the use of his products or services. He interests the prospect by telling him how the product can improve his own product quality, reduce waste, or speed up production in his factory. Having gained some interest by using broad benefits, the salesman can then continue the interview successfully to a point where he can suggest his product to solve a specific problem.

In the foregoing example, the salesman actually got his prospect's interest in the approach statement by mentioning the system that he had sold to the prospect's neighbor, Dick Brown. In many creative selling situations, he may not have the advantage of such a referral installation. He may have to concentrate on getting attention without really knowing whether there is justifiable interest in his products. How does he find out? Here are some of the things the salesman might do to arouse interest:

> *Salesman:* "Mr. Jones, I'd like to tell you about some of the typical applications for this recorder in a lab like yours, and also to mention some of the specific benefits in terms of performance, versatility, reliability, and economy which prompted these customers to switch to ABC."

Here the salesman used the possible application and suggested benefit approach to arouse interest. Another common method would be to ask questions during the course of the demonstration to determine such things as the extent of recorder usage in the lab, the present brand standardization, the specific appeal of your product feature – benefit claims, the likelihood of a new or replacement requirement, and the like. It would be futile, indeed, to expect to create desire for your product unless there is evidence of interest.

30

Desire

This is the most important — and usually the most difficult to accomplish — of the steps leading to a creative sale. Here the salesman must

present benefit points in a deliberate, clear, and skillful manner. The prospect will desire the product only when he believes its use will benefit him. The specific value of such benefits must be explained thoroughly and in such a manner as to remove all doubts about the validity of such claims. If the salesman fails to do this, doubts will arise in the prospect's mind and sometimes orders are lost. The prospect wants assurance that the product will do what the salesman says, and that it will produce the benefits he needs in solving his specific problem. Finally, the prospect will want to know who else uses it? May I see one? How much does it cost? At this stage, desire is reaching a peak and it is the salesman's job to turn this strong desire into a buying decision.

The rate of progress toward the sale normally slows down at this point while the prospect deliberates the pros and cons of the one or more proposals under consideration. It is at this point that competition may be invited, and, as a result, the prospect may have doubts about which product to purchase. Frequent follow-up contacts by the salesman may be necessary to determine whether such doubts have arisen and, if so, to eliminate them by positive proof.

Decision

This step is the last step before obtaining the order. Perhaps it should be called favorable decision because only a favorable decision will lead to an order. The accomplishment of this step requires a logical and skillful summarization of the most convincing arguments.

31

DECISION *is achieved...*

The salesman should have questioned extensively to identify the major deterrents to getting an order. To make a successful close, the salesman must emotionally move the prospect to place his order. The specific techniques used will depend on a recognition by the salesman of the important obstacles involved. Good judgment and, to some extent, intuition will determine the order-closing techniques to be used.

Suggested Self-Development Exercises

This explanation of the steps to a sale has been given largely for identification purpose to make the salesman conscious of them so that he may appraise his progress in making a sale. The salesman should devote some time to interpreting these steps in the context of his own products and selling situation by doing the following:

1. Prepare in readily referable and usable form a refined check list of all the pre-approach duties which might have to be performed in advance of a creative or prospective sales call. Following this, he should place a check mark identifying those duties which are usually necessary in preparation for the normal follow-up sales call.
2. For practice, it would be well to write several statements which have been used successfully in accomplishing each of the following steps to a sale: Pre-approach, Approach, Attention, Interest, and Desire. This exercise invariably results in stronger selling statements and more effective presentations.

How the Steps to a Sale are Accomplished

The positive influences by which the steps to a sale are accomplished can be analyzed and delineated in specific and understandable terms, and the negative influences which may impede or block the progress of a sale can be identified as specific obstacles.

The means by which the salesman accomplishes these steps and overcomes these obstacles are the selling tools. The understanding, selection, and skillful use of the selling tools is essential, but many salesmen do not recognize or identify the tools which they work with daily. Most salesmen use them subconsciously without full realization of their most advantageous and timely application.

The Selling Tools

The salesman has at his disposal 13 selling tools, each of which has a particular purpose and effect in accomplishing the steps to a sale or in overcoming the obstacles to a sale. Each tool is designed to

SALES TOOLS	
Customer Benefits	Assurance
Loss	Sales Stories
Product Qualities	Free Service
Competitive	Contact
Poor Qualities	Atmosphere
Prestige	Questions
Pride	Good Judgment

accomplish a specific result. The appropriate selection and use of each tool may be planned in advance, and it may be used with full confidence that it will accomplish its intended purpose.

Everything that the salesman says or does in his efforts to make a sale can be classified under one of these 13 selling tool categories. Similarly, the wording of an advertisement, or the content of a sales letter, must contain these same selling tools, if they are to be effective. It is, therefore, essential that each tool be clearly understood in terms of the salesman's particular products or services. The knowledge of what the sales tools are and what they can accomplish will not in itself assure success.

Most important is the development of skill in the selection and use of these tools. To do this effectively will involve considerable effort by the salesman. He must discipline himself always to analyze what he says and does in terms of these tools.

Many of these selling tools, particularly those that have emotional appeal, are applicable to one's daily social life, although they are normally used subconsciously, and all of the tools are used in consumer and commercial product sales promotion. The salesman should form the habit of identifying and observing the use of selling tools in advertisements and radio and TV commercials. Such an analysis will reveal why certain promotional efforts are particularly successful.

The selling tools are:

1. Customer benefits
2. Product qualities
3. Competitive poor qualities
4. Loss
5. Prestige
6. Pride

7. Assurance
8. Story
9. Service
10. Contact
11. Atmosphere
12. Wedge questions

13. Good judgment

It is interesting to note that of the 13 selling tools, eight represent appeals to logic, and five represent appeals to the emotions. The logic tools are customer benefits, product qualities, competitive poor qualities, loss, assurance, service, wedge questions, and good judgment, and the emotional tools are prestige, pride, story, contact, and atmosphere. This breakdown points out that people buy for both logical and emotional reasons. In technical selling, the logic influences may appear to be most significant, but, in fact, appeals to emotion contribute greatly to motivate a favorable buying decision.

CUSTOMER BENEFITS

This is the most important of all the selling tools. These are the advantages which your prospect will gain from your products or

services. To a manufacturer, such benefits may include savings in production costs or production time, improvement to his product, and many others. To an individual, they may include such things as improvement of his health, protection of his family, improvement of his mind, and countless other benefits. Consumer benefits are absolutely essential to create interest, build desire, and bring about a favorable buying decision. Benefits answer the biggest question in the prospect's mind — one which stands in the way of every creative sale — "What can the product do for me?" They are the prime reason for buying the product. It is, therefore, important to develop, and have available, a list of customer benefits which relate specifically to your products.

PRODUCT QUALITIES

Product qualities are those characteristics or features of the product or service which make it superior. They relate to design, con-

should be translated into benefits

struction, performance, appearance, durability, reliability, and maintenance. The most important product qualities are those that relate directly to customer benefits.

The product quality selling tool is probably one of the most used and also most abused. Many sales presentations, trade paper advertisements, and sales letters stress and emphasize product qualities without direct reference to the resulting consumer benefits. They assume that the prospect will immediately recognize or infer the practical benefits of these features, although many times he may not do so.

Another common fault is to mention too many product qualities, some of which may have little, if any, significant benefit value. The salesman should never mention a product quality without relating it to the customer benefit it produces.

DEVELOPING A TYPICAL PRODUCT PROFILE

A typical example of the product profile is shown in the accompanying illustration, which refers to a laboratory recorder. This type of tabulation should be done for each major product by first listing all of the features of the product which might possibly be considered important product qualities. This should be done without regard for their relative degree of importance. A separate listing should be made of all the conceivable benefits which might possibly result

PRODUCT QUALITIES (Features)	Accuracy	Speed	Reliability	Economy	Ease of Maintenance	Durability	Time-Labor Cost Savings	Flexibility	Product Improvement
			CUSTOMER BENEFITS						
Sensitivity -Resolution	X								X
Calibration -Rangeability -Suppression		X					X	X	
Solid Circuitry			X	X	X	X			
Ground Isolation	X								
Chart Speed Adjustment		X					X	X	
Power Requirements				X					
Signal to Noise Ratio	X								
Mechanical Features			X		X	X			

PRODUCT PROFILE

from the utilization of the product by the customer. From these lists, a product profile should be prepared which will serve to identify the more important product qualities in terms of directly related benefits. It may also be used as a basis for composing effective selling statements. However, the product profile is merely a work sheet which should not be used in this form for visual presentation to a customer. Preparing this work sheet is a necessary step to the development of powerful selling statements and acquiring skill in using them in any form of sales presentation.

COMPETITIVE POOR QUALITIES

Competitive poor qualities represent weaknesses in the competitive products. These may be weaknesses in design, construction, appearance, reliability which make them inferior. Another interpretation of competitive poor qualities may be the use of a conventional

1. Limited Product Line

2. Lack of Engineering Service

3. Wider Manufacturing Tolerances

or technically outmoded method of doing something compared with an advanced method which is offered in the salesman's more modern products. Competitive poor qualities are used to contrast and emphasize product qualities. They are usually mentioned in the same statement or paragraph as the product good qualities and customer benefits. Competitive poor qualities must always be used in straightforward comparisons, and they should be used discretely. Skillful salesmen refrain from mentioning competitors by name and, of course, they never knock or malign competitors directly.

It is important that the salesman become thoroughly familiar with the products of his principal competitors. He should understand their claims and he should evaluate them objectively and realistically, thus preparing himself in the event the prospect should challenge him on a competitor's superior performance claim. Both the good qualities and poor qualities of the competitor's products must be carefully analyzed and counter statements, together with a plan of rebuttal, should be developed in anticipation of possible use during the sales presentation.

Loss

Loss points frequently make good order closers. They are used to further emphasize competitive poor qualities or to dramatize the undesirable consequences which may result from not using your products. This may be done by using competitive products, or by using out-moded methods of measurement or analysis for which your products offer a superior solution. Loss points should be stated in factual terms such as dollar loss, time loss, loss of profits, or production delays. Loss points, stated factually, dramatize customer benefits, because most salesmen claim benefits for their products, and the prospect becomes accustomed to vague claims. The prospect

is more likely to be impressed by loss points that emphasize waste or out-of-pocket costs to him.

The following example shows how to use customer benefits, product qualities, competitive poor qualities, and loss as tools in a creative selling situation:

Salesman Smith: "Mr. Jones, there are some major criteria that everyone uses in selecting recording equipment. For example, you want accuracy, flexibility, reliability, economy of operation and this recorder has been developed with these important benefits in mind.

"The 20-foot, multi-convolution slide wire ensures maximum sensitivity and accuracy. This accuracy is further safeguarded by unique ground isolation circuitry that maximizes the signal-to-noise ratio and assures constant usable accuracy under a wide range of operating conditions. These features are unique and not available on any other recorders.

"Extreme flexibility is made possible by this 12-step range calibration and suppression switching arrangement, which permits you to use the recorder for many more applications, and it may save you money by eliminating the need for several special purpose recorders.

"The solid circuitry used throughout this new design increases reliability, thereby avoiding costly shut-downs during critical test runs. Without this feature and its compact design, a conventional recorder could not be mounted in your standard relay racks.

"You don't usually think of operating economy in selecting recorders, but this can become very important when you need to make multiple copies of the chart record. With this new pressurized inking feature, you get records which can be repro-

39

duced instantly using your standard copying equipment. There is no need to go through the costly, time-consuming steps of making negatives and photo reproductions, as you do with many other recorders. Just think of the money you'll save by up-dating your method!"

Suggested Self-Development Exercises

Do the following exercise in order to understand the use of these first four tools. Interpret them in terms of your own products.

1. Write examples of customer benefits and product qualities for several products.
2. Prepare product profiles for two typical, but different, products which you handle.
3. List examples of competitive poor qualities for products of two important competitors. These should preferably relate to products included in the product profile.
4. Write examples of loss points relating to customer benefits from number 1.
5. Write selling statements or paragraphs which use customer benefits, product qualities, competitive poor qualities, and loss as sales tools.

PRESTIGE

This selling tool is designed to build confidence in your company, in its products, or in you as a company representative. When trying to

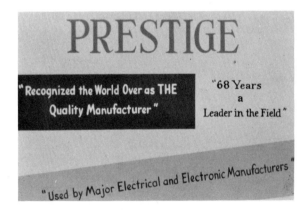

make a creative sale prestige may be important in gaining and holding the prospect's attention.

Typical prestige statements convey impressions of capability,

40

depth of experience, length of service, achievements, and, in general, the reputation which you, your staff or your company possess. You use a personal prestige tool when you say to your prospect, "I've been selling and applying these products in your industry for the last ten years." Typical company prestige statements include the following: "My company has been in this business since 1900 and it has pioneered most of the important advances in our industry." "There are more of my company's products used in your industry today than all other makes combined."

Prestige selling tools should be used discretely in order to avoid the impression of bragging. Companies use them widely in blue-chip and horizontal or industry-wide publications to build a favorable image. Used alone, they do not make the sale, but they are invaluable in getting attention and helping the prospect make a decision.

PRIDE

This can be the most effective of the five selling tools that appeal to the emotions. It has wide application both in business and social contacts.

Pride tools are those which convey, in a sincere manner, an appreciation and recognition of the prospect's ability, character, reputation, and accomplishments. They may be applied to the individual, his family, home or hobby. They can be equally effective when applied to the prospect's company, its products, services, and reputation. The purpose of pride tools is to make the prospect feel kindly toward you—to make him like to talk to and deal with you because you make him feel good.

The manner in which you use this tool and the circumstances and timing of its application are extremely important. If the pride tool is used excessively or inopportunely, it may be interpreted as flattery

flattery will get you nowhere!

and thereby create a negative impression. Do not confuse pride with flattery, and always use the pride tool with sincerity and discretion. It will benefit you, especially when it's applied during the approach and attention steps to a sale. The following are some examples of how a salesman can use this pride tool:

"What a nice photograph! Are those your children? You sure have a good looking family!"

"That's an attractive trophy." "Is golfing one of your hobbies? Where did you win it?"

"You certainly have an attractive new plant. This picture gives a better impression of its size and efficient layout. This must have taken lots of careful planning and hard work on your part!"

"That's a dandy model of your new jet engine. I've been reading your recent ads and it sure sounds like a real performer! How is it being received by the industry?"

In these examples, the salesman used the pride tool in four distinctly different ways—the personal family compliment, the personal sports achievement recognition, the new plant mentioned, and finally the new-product comment. Obviously, he would not have used all of these in the same interview. Normally one would serve the desired purpose which is to warm up the prospect and make him want to talk to you.

ASSURANCE

Assurance selling tools are employed to instill confidence and trust in your prospect's mind. The obvious examples of the assurance selling tools are user lists, installation references, testimonial letters and advertisements, guarantees, and personal references. These are all used widely but in many instances they are used in a perfunctory or

routine manner and thus have minimal impact on the prospect. You can increase their effectiveness by carefully constructing the variations of this tool and by using them selectively to suit the specific selling problem. For example, a photograph album showing typical installations and augmented by pertinent comments is much more impressive than handing out, or reciting, a list of users. A specific, closely related application reference becomes more potent when you arrange for your prospect to visit the installation in person. Testimonial letters and personal references are most effective when they are supplemented by a direct telephone conversation between your prospect and the satisfied user. Advertisements mean more when they spell out and dramatize specific customer benefits and averted losses and the savings which result.

STORY

The story selling tool has two major purposes. The first is to provide some relaxation or change of pace during an intense or concentrated sales interview or product demonstration. It may be used to avoid boredom on the part of the prospect and also to restore his complete concentration on and attention to your mission.

The second purpose is to emphasize, in a subtle manner, the important selling tools like customer benefits, product qualities, loss points, or service.

An effective story tool should comprise an interesting account of an actual experience which some other customer has had with your products. For maximum effectiveness, the story should have some novelty and human interest qualities, and, hopefully, it should also relate in some way to your prospect's business interest in your products.

To ensure maximum impact, the story should be told skillfully, dramatizing where possible. Supporting visual evidence such as a

43

keep a mental file of SALES STORIES

photograph, chart record or trade paper clipping is desirable. These stories should be thought out in advance and they should be rehearsed to assure a smooth, understandable and interesting presentation. The salesman should develop a mental file of such stories in sufficient variety to apply to a broad spectrum of industries and product applications. They are most helpful when used during the desire and decision steps to a sale, because they serve to confirm benefit claims.

Suggested Self-Development Exercises

PRESTIGE

1. Make a list of all of the company prestige points that you can think of.
2. Study these carefully and indicate by number their relative effectiveness based on your own judgment.
3. Compose and write sentences embodying the more important company prestige points. These should be written in the same manner as you would speak them to a prospect.
4. List prestige points relative to yourself.
5. Compose and write sentences which will convey these personal prestige points discretely to your prospect.

PRIDE

1. Consider how you now utilize the pride tool in your daily customer contacts. Do you use it to best advantage? Do you use it skillfully?
2. Write several typical examples of how you can apply the pride tool to your prospect personally, and to your prospect's company or its products.

ASSURANCE

1. List all the things that your company provides and which may serve you as assurance selling tools.

44

2. Make a similar list of the assurance tools that can be particularly effective in your own sales territory.
3. How do you think the assurance tools can be used to maximum advantage in the steps to a sale?

STORY

1. Write a synopsis of three stories which fit the definition of this selling tool. These should be based on your own selling experience.
2. Do you need additional stories based on the experiences of the other salesmen to augment your own collection? If so, get them and use them as your own.
3. How do you use the story sales tool to the best advantage?

GENERAL

1. Review several trade magazines—preferably those related to your type products and markets—and clip out six or more typical product advertisements that catch your eye.
2. Analyze these ads and identify, by number, the selling tools that are used. These are sure to contain some of the first eight tools that you have studied. Some will contain the remaining five tools.

SERVICE

Service comprises all of those things which you or your company may do for your prospect and his company free of charge. They may include such things as application, engineering advice and assistance, help in checking out and starting up a new installation, no-charge warranty repair service, product training for your customers' technicians on either a cost or no charge basis, free operating demonstrations, trial installations of your product in his plant, educational

be ready with
FREE SERVICE

bulletins issued periodically. Many companies publish house organs which contain interesting examples of how other companies use their products or comments on important changes in the trade.

In addition to these typical, definable services, there are numerous instances where the salesman performs a personal service for his customer. Publicizing a technical accomplishment falls into this category. Other personal services include such things as obtaining tickets for a sports event or a show. Some discrete forms of entertainment fall in this category.

Most companies offer some free services but they often fail to capitalize on them in not making sure that the customer recognizes them and appreciates their worth. Service tools may be used to excellent advantage during the interest and decision steps to a sale. The salesman should always include them in his summary of advantages and competitive comparisons when attempting to close a sale. He should never assume that the customer will give these unusual services full consideration in making the buying decision.

If your company offers a substantial number of these service tools—hopefully in greater measure than your competitors do—you may indeed be fortunate. By appropriately stressing these free services, you may well be able to use them to justify and off-set minor price disadvantages.

CONTACT

The purpose of contact tools is to quickly establish a closer relationship with the prospect or customer. Many people are reserved when they meet a stranger for the first time. And this attitude might be more prevalent in the mind of the prospect or customer who grants an audience to a salesman. Contact tools help to identify the salesman as a person and to facilitate a warm and more intimate personal relationship.

don't overlook CONTACT

This tool can be extremely helpful to the salesman on a prospecting sales call. It can be equally helpful when calling for the first time on new employees of established customers. When making a prospecting call, the use of a contact tool in arranging an appointment may be essential to getting an interview. When a cold call is attempted without an appointment, a good contact reference can be a reliable door opener. Contact tools should always be used during the pre-approach step to a sale.

Using the name of a mutual friend or acquaintance in opening an initial interview is a typical example of the contact selling tool. Mention of some mutual interests like professional or trade association activities, school associations, hobbies or sports may provide a similar effect.

The experienced salesman habitually searches for contact points in advance of making a prospecting call or prior to visiting a new customer. This involves learning all that he possibly can from all available sources about the people and the company he plans to see. When the salesman has difficulty in finding an appropriate contact reference to suit the requirement, it will pay him to check with his supervisor or with his home office for help in this connection. A discreet approach through the sales department might serve your purpose by arranging for the desired introductions.

Contact tools are most useful in the approach and attention steps to a sale and they can be most effective when their use is anticipated and planned in advance of the sales call.

ATMOSPHERE

This selling tool comprises all of the personal and environmental factors that may influence the prospect's impressions or that may enhance, or adversely affect, the salesman's progress and the effectiveness of the sales call. In the personal category are the salesman's

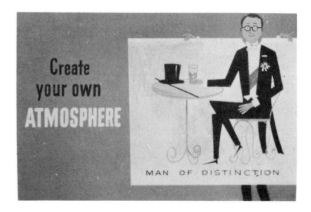

appearance or dress, and his mood or manner. Certainly conservatism, good taste, and neatness in dress are essential. Loud, gaudy, excessively informal or other unconventional attire may arouse suspicions and create unfavorable impressions in the prospect's mind. Casual, unconventional attire has its place, of course, but this should not be in the customer's office.

The salesman's outward personality manifestations are even more important. His mood or manner should convey enthusiasm, alertness, and vitality. A smile, and a friendly, sincere manner are essential and they are to some extent contagious because they can warm up the prospect and make him enjoy talking with you. The typical salesman's inner mood cannot always reflect these personality attributes, but, like a good actor, he should never convey such negative moods or feelings to the prospect through outward appearance or personality manifestations. The salesman should take a good look at himself in a full length mirror before starting to make calls each day and he should try to be objectively critical of what he sees. The rest is up to him.

The physical or environmental interpretations of the atmosphere selling tool are obvious and they can contribute or detract from the effectiveness of the sales interview. These may include the physical surroundings or locale where the interview is conducted. The prospect's private office or conference room which is free from interruptions or other distracting influences is the preferred place to conduct the sales interview or the product demonstration. The reception lobby, or general office area or a noisy factory bench can detract seriously from the effectiveness of the call. Fortunately, these factors are to a large extent controllable. Good advance planning and arrangements in the pre-approach step can do much to ensure a favorable physical environment in which to conduct the sales interview or product demonstration. If this cannot be done in advance, the salesman must try during the approach and attention steps to influence the customer to arrange the interview or demonstration in a place free from interruptions. There may be instances when the salesman may have to utilize his own office or a near-by hotel room for such a demonstration or sales presentation to do it most effectively.

The last working edge of the atmosphere tool is time or timing. A good salesman is conscious of this when he selects the most opportune time to talk to the prospect—a time when he may be free from interruptions and be in a more receptive frame of mind. Unfortunately, there is no such thing as an ideal time to make the sales contact. This may vary widely depending on the duties and work routine of the prospect. Consideration should always be given to the prospect's situation and point of view. For example, it is highly unlikely that a successful and fully cooperative interview can be accomplished late in the working day when the customer may be under pressure to complete essential chores which have accumulated during the day. There are occasions when appointments after work may be practical and welcomed by the extremely busy individual.

When atmosphere conditions — environmental, personal or timing — are unfavorable, it may be preferable not to press for an important sales presentation or demonstration at the time. The atmosphere tool is of paramount importance during the attention and interest steps to a sale.

WEDGE QUESTIONS

If a successful, experienced salesman were asked to assign some order of priority or relative importance to the 13 selling tools, it is likely that wedge questions would rate near the top, second only to customer benefits. The purpose of such questions is to get information. To the salesman questions are an indispensable tool because he is always seeking information. This is true throughout five of the steps to a sale, from approach to decision.

In the early steps, he urgently needs information about the prospect's use of or need for his type of products, his prospect's buying habits, his current and future requirements, identification of the people who influence the selection and purchase and many other things. If there is a requirement, and the salesman has been able to arouse interest and some degree of desire for his products, it would be that he must find out how he stands with respect to his competitor. He must determine from the prospect the strengths and weaknesses of his company's proposal versus his competition in order to determine the most effective order closing strategy and thus obtain a favorable buying decision.

Much of this critical information is not volunteered by the prospect and if the competition is strongly favored, it may be very difficult to obtain this information by normal means. That is why this selling tool is called Wedge Questions. These questions must be carefully phrased and skillfully used to obtain urgently needed information. These are custom-designed questions and should not be confused with conventional questions that are commonly asked. Conventional questions, when asked bluntly, or in great abundance or frequency, may cause the prospect to clam up.

There are three broad categories of wedge questions:

1. Investigation questions get basic background information essential to making an appropriate and effective sales presentation. Some of the important facts needed include the company's usage or needs for the salesman's products, the prospect's product preferences and buying habits, his current or probable future requirements, identification of the several people who may influence the selection and purchase, and the competitive situation.
2. Suggestion questions tactfully and unobtrusively plant favorable ideas in the prospect's mind. This is done most successfully when it plants a thought which the prospect assumes he originated himself.
3. Test questions check the progress and effectiveness of the salesman's presentation and, most important, evaluate his chances of getting the order.

The salesman should interpret these three categories in terms of his own products and selling conditions. He should then create, write, and try questions in these three categories. Conscientious effort will improve the salesman's skill and, consequently, his sales.

It is of utmost importance to consider carefully the prospect's responses — after the interview. Jot them down in a pocket memo book. These responses must be analyzed carefully, because they may contain clues to the prospect's preferences.

Here's how a salesman can make use of these wedge questions.

Salesman Smith: "Mr. Jones, you have a large heat treating department here, about how many furnaces do you have? Do you use recorders and controllers on all of them?"

This is a typical example of an investigation type of wedge question. The salesman was making an initial call on his prospect who is in charge of instrumentation in an automotive heat treating department. This is representative of the common straightforward question used to get basic information which is not classified or restricted. This is the simplest form of question. Be careful to avoid asking too many pointed questions and thus turn the interview into an inquisition. Some prospects thoroughly enjoy answering such questions and even volunteer to expand on them. Others may have a tendency to be more secretive and they may "clam up" when pressed for too much information. The salesman must carefully observe his prospect's reaction to the questioning and judge how far he should go in pressing for this information. Here is another type of question.

> Salesman Smith: "I am impressed by the large number of recorders that you use in the laboratories. Is the operating cost an important consideration? Do you have to reproduce chart records frequently? Then you will be interested in this new pressurized inking feature which provides records that can be reproduced instantly using your standard available copying equipment. Just think what this can save you in time and materials!"

Here the salesman used a suggestion-type question. He mentioned operating costs and got a confirmation that these were important considerations in selecting recorders. He then proceeded to mention a particular feature of his recorder — pressurized inking — which makes more economical chart reproduction. Doubtless he will stress this further in his product demonstration. Later he would further emphasize this benefit by suggesting possible loss in dollars that results from the present uneconomical record reproducing methods.

> Salesman Smith: "Mr. Jones, now that you have seen this new recorder in operation and have observed its several superior features, do you agree that these can be of real benefit to you? Would you like to try one out in your plant?"

The test question which Smith used here had the obvious intent to measure prospect Jones's reactions and impressions of the new recorder. Undoubtedly the salesman would watch carefully during the demonstration to note the reactions to his product quality-customer benefit claims, and he would want some positive indication of the total impact of his demonstration.

The salesman should prepare statements in these three categories which relate to his products and are more pertinent to his specific selling situation.

GOOD JUDGMENT

Experience can, and does, contribute immeasurably to the development of good judgment, but experience is not, in itself, the most important ingredient. There is much more involved in acquiring good selling judgment. This may be defined as the acumen or insight which the salesman must exercise in conscientiously and continuously utilizing the previously defined 12 selling tools for maximum advantage and effectiveness. Good selling judgment is actually the result of careful planning and analysis of the selling problem.

A salesman helps to develop good judgment when he forms the habit of being analytical and objectively critical while progressing through the steps to a sale. When he loses an order he must try to determine the reasons. This may be a painful and sometimes embarrassing exercise but it enables him to get the maximum benefit from his unsuccessful experience. This is the surest way to develop good judgment in the selling profession.

Suggested Self-Development Exercises

SERVICE

1. Make a list of all of the free services which your company offers.
2. Study these services and then rearrange them in order of their relative importance, based on your own judgment.
3. Compose and write down sentences embodying the more important service tools.

CONTACT

1. Consider, then write, the best sources of contacts for use on initial sales calls.
2. Write several statements using the contact tool in various selling situations.

ATMOSPHERE

    1. List the more critical personal manifestations of this tool.

    2. Describe techniques which you have used successfully to ensure satisfactory environmental conditions.

WEDGE QUESTIONS

    1. Write three examples, based on your own experience, of effective wedge questions in each of the following categories:

       A. Investigation
       B. Suggestion
       C. Test

The responses to the Service and Wedge Questions exercises can make valuable additions to your permanent sales manual.

The Product Demonstration

The 13 selling tools cover all of the positive influences that constitute the steps to a sale and help to get the order. The two greatest personal rewards that the sales engineer can receive are the order and the satisfaction and pleasure that come from a well-planned and skillfully executed product demonstration.

The product demonstration is a very essential part of the sales presentation. It can be an enjoyable experience for the salesman, and an interesting and rewarding experience for the prospect. The product demonstration carries a powerful selling impact because it conveys audio-visual impressions. The demonstration provides some opportunity for showmanship and ego nourishment. The alert and discerning salesman observes his audience carefully during the demonstration and he can sense impressions and reactions. Favorable reactions usually result in orders and personal satisfaction resulting from a job well done.

Product demonstrations are made for several reasons: to give the salesman a foundation on which to build his sales presentation, to focus the prospect's attention on the sales story, to demonstrate superior product performance, and to show the product-operating principle that allows certain customer benefits.

Planning the demonstration and developing the actual demonstration procedure should be similar to the total sales planning effort, and the same steps-to-a-sale techniques should be applied.

Under pre-approach will be the preliminaries such as checking over the demonstrator and conducting a practice demonstration run. Where to go, whom to see, making the appointment, are also included here.

The approach functions are also similar. The salesman should arrive at the prospect's company at least 30 minutes early to make sure that the meeting room is appropriate and to set up and check out the demonstrator. It is desirable to have someone at the company you are visiting to assist you with this preparation and, more important, to assist in rounding up all of the influential people who should witness the demonstration. Always keep in mind the importance of first impressions. Both you and your product should be ready, able, and fully prepared to put on an interesting and stimulating presentation.

The demonstration itself substantially accomplishes the attention step but this should not be taken for granted. When demonstrating to a group, keep in mind the interests of the various individuals and to identify features and benefits which may have specific individual appeal. Attention may be sustained by getting the prospect involved in the demonstration. Have him personally operate the equipment to show a particular feature. Directing suggestion and test-type wedge questions to the prospect will also help to sustain his attention.

The interest step comprises pitching your demonstration in terms of the particular applications and performance requirements of the prospect. Frequent reference to the prospect's problems with explanation as to how your product qualities may alleviate them is of course desirable. Customer benefits which may be directly pertinent should be identified in broad terms early in the demonstration.

The desire and decision steps comprise the heart of the demonstration. This is where the customer benefits are further explained and proven by reference to significant product qualities or features. The operating demonstration should be conducted as simply as possible and the technical explanation should be elementary to make sure that the prospect will understand. In a group demonstration, complex technical questions should be politely and discretely deferred for individual handling following the operating demonstration. Interruptions for inconsequential reasons should be avoided.

It is most important that the demonstration plan or outline be followed explicitly, regardless of interruptions or diversions. An orderly summary should always be included at the close of the demonstration. Reference should again be made to the important customer benefits, stressing briefly the superior product qualities which make these benefits possible.

The summary statement should include the use of assurance tools such as user references, warranty back-up. Service tools should also be used again to identify the free, supporting services which the salesman and his company offer to make sure that the prospect will obtain maximum value from his investment.

How much effort the salesman makes to accomplish a favorable buying decision will depend upon the circumstances which led up to the demonstration meeting. If an active competitive procurement is involved, based on quotations submitted earlier, a strong order closing attempt should be made. If the circumstances make it impossible or impracticable to close the order at this time, a strong effort should be made to obtain some kind of commitment from the prospect. Such a commitment may consist of a trial installation, a visit to a nearby installation for reference purposes, an opportunity to write or revise the purchase requisition specifications, or to lay out the installation in anticipation for an imminent order. In many sales presentations, the demonstration provides an excellent buying decision or order-closing opportunity.

It is good practice to leave some reminder with each member of the audience. This may be a catalog, an appropriate application bulletin, or a product photograph to which is attached a one-page product profile, listing the product qualities and customer benefits. It is also recommended that each demonstration be followed-up by a phone call or a personal call at an early date. The purpose of this is to get some action whether it be an order or approval for a trial installation. The following check list provides a guide for the salesman in arranging the demonstration of his own products.

PREPARATION

1. Check the demonstrator under operating conditions before leaving the office.
2. Review and rehearse the demonstration procedure.
3. Bring a supply of applicable literature.
4. Make the appointment arrangements carefully to insure getting the influential people in an appropriate atmosphere at the right time.
5. Arrive early enough to set up and operate the demonstrator in advance, and to round up the influential personnel.

INTRODUCTORY COMMENTS

6. Identify yourself, your company and the product to be demonstrated.
7. Point out the relationship between your product and the prospect's business.
8. Briefly review the pertinent customer benefits which your product makes possible and mention that the product qualities or features which contribute to these benefits will be pointed out during the operating demonstration.

9. Invite questions and individual participation during the demonstration.

10. Operate the demonstrator and, if possible, simulate and talk in terms of the prospect's application problems throughout the presentation.
11. Explain the fundamental operating principles in simple technical language.
12. Point out the important product quality features, one-by-one and identify the customer benefits which each one contributes.
13. Dramatize the demonstration procedure where practical to emphasize such things as speed, sensitivity, safety, and reliability capability.
14. Invite individual participation or manipulation of the demonstrator if this is practical.
15. Relax the prospect by telling an interesting story of another customer's experience which illustrates in a dramatic manner one of the benefits claimed for your product.
16. Be sure to complete the planned demonstration procedure, adhering to the anticipated time schedule.

THE CONCLUSION

17. Summarize the presentation by deliberately referring to the customer benefits claimed in the introductory comments. Again, briefly identify the product qualities or features which support these benefit claims. Hand out a product profile sheet or suitable alternative literature.
18. Point out typical users and suggest a personal visit to verify the performance and reliability claims which have been made.
19. Mention the free services which you and your company provide to assure lasting customer satisfaction and maximum return from the investment.
20. Make an appropriate order closing or decision effort which will result in some form of commitment by the prospect.

The Obstacles to a Sale

Considerable space has been devoted in the preceding pages to a description of the selling tools—the positive elements of selling—which cover everything the salesman can do, write, or say to influ-

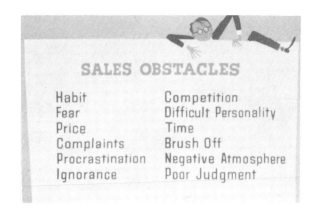

SALES OBSTACLES

Habit	Competition
Fear	Difficult Personality
Price	Time
Complaints	Brush Off
Procrastination	Negative Atmosphere
Ignorance	Poor Judgment

ence the prospect and accomplish a sale. Unfortunately, the progress toward a sale is not always positive and smooth and obstacles do present themselves in most, if not all, sales situations.

The appropriate and timely selection and use of the selling tools can prevent or overcome objections and other forms of obstacles which may otherwise impede or prevent the sale. Frequently, the prospect does not voluntarily express his objections and the salesman may not realize that any obstacles exist. It is extremely important that the presence of such obstacles or objections be detected as early in the interview as possible. The wedge question selling tool can accomplish this for the salesman if he will use it in a timely and skillful manner.

Most of the obstacles which the salesman normally encounters can be categorized under the following 12 headings:

1. Habit	7. Competition
2. Fear	8. Difficult Personality
3. Price	9. Time
4. Complaints	10. Brush-off
5. Procrastination	11. Negative atmosphere
6. Ignorance	12. Poor judgment

HABIT

Many people have a tendency to resist change despite the fact that change may be for the better. This is particularly true when the prospect has had some degree of success with a product or with a method of solving a measurement or control problem. The situation is usually more acute when the prospect has pioneered the use of the competitive product or the now outmoded method or procedure. In this case, he may resist new and better ways of doing things. Habit, then, becomes an obstacle when the prospect refuses the salesman's

recognize the
HABIT obstacle

product or service because he is accustomed to other products or methods.

Wedge questions should be used to discover the presence and depth of the prospect's habit. The salesman should listen carefully to the prospect's point of view and to his reasoning. If the habit is causing some definable sacrifice, the salesman should point this out using loss to support customer benefit claims. The application of these tools is always beneficial. Frequently, pride can be used in a subtle manner by complimenting the prospect on his earlier foresight in making the initial selection and by implying renewed recognition from his management for adopting a superior, more modern product or method.

FEAR

Fear is a potent obstacle in selling to the consumer. A consumer has an instinctive fear that he may be high-pressured into buying something he doesn't need or he fears the unpleasantness of turning the salesman away and refusing to buy from him.

In selling to industry, the fear obstacle may be present in several forms. The prospect may be fearful that by purchasing the salesman's product or service he may later be subjected to criticism from his management. The reasons behind this form of obstacle must be determined. Possible reasons may include: breaking down standardization of another make of product thereby causing extra spare parts and maintenance expense; failure to obtain the alleged pay-out for the capital investment involved; unfavorable union reaction to a labor saving product or system; and hesitancy in asking for the necessary money appropriation.

Assurance and customer benefits are effective in combatting this form of fear. Testimonials, user lists, visits or telephone checks with nearby users can overcome this obstacle.

Another common manifestation of the fear obstacle concerns the

FEAR needs assurance

salesman himself. The new salesman may be fearful in approaching a new prospect or in pressing to see all of the individuals who might influence the buying decision. He may be fearful of handling a violent customer complaint. To overcome this fear, the salesman must have complete confidence in his products and the benefits which they can contribute. He must also have the intestinal fortitude to tell his well prepared story to everyone involved.

PRICE

Although price is not often an obstacle in creative industrial selling, it frequently is in negotiated, competitive sales. Price cutting is a common last resort of the competitor who suffers some disadvantages (i.e. lack of comparable features, performance, reliability, poor delivery, etc.). Frequently, the value offered by the low priced competitor is inferior and in such a situation the salesman must point this out in a clear but discrete manner. If the competitor's value is fully equivalent then it may be that the salesman's price structure is at

...must be outweighed by benefits

fault. A universal answer to the price obstacle is to summarize and emphasize all of the applicable selling tools, stressing, where practicable, service or other pertinent advantages.

The price obstacle may be present when there is no competition. In such situations, the prospect may feel that the advantages of using the salesman's product or system do not justify the costs involved. When this objection is raised, the salesman must courteously and patiently probe the economic analysis supporting this opinion and try again to justify his price, giving concrete examples of money saving benefits supported by the experience of other users. As a last resort, and if company policy permits, a trial installation, conditional sale or leasing arrangement may be negotiated.

COMPLAINTS

There are occasions when the salesman is unable to get the prospect's favorable attention because of some former mistreatment,

COMPLAINTS must be dealt with

which may have involved such things as product difficulties, poor deliveries, slow communications, or other faults.

When attempting to overcome a complaint, there are several fundamental techniques which should be used. The first is to listen attentively and sympathetically to all of the details. The salesman should then suggest corrective actions or give reassurance that there will be no recurrence or further cause for complaint.

The salesman should never directly condemn his company or specific individuals who were involved in the incident. Such negative strategy may further confirm the customer's unfavorable impressions. In difficult situations, it may be desirable to provide further reassurance by letter or a visit from an official from the salesman's home office.

PROCRASTINATION

Procrastination is another prevalent human obstacle which the salesman must contend with. The prospect delays making a decision or taking prompt action, in spite of his apparent desire for the product or service. His inaction may be caused by the extra effort which he will have to exert to justify the expenditure, initiate the purchase order, and then follow through with installation details when delivery is made.

The salesman should utilize wedge questions to try to determine the specific cause for the procrastination. It may be that the salesman can offer to assist in the accomplishment of details like preparing an expenditure justification, laying out or supervising the installation of the product, or arranging special training for the customer's personnel.

Stressing customer benefits and contrasting loss is always good strategy and may serve to make the causes for the customer's procrastination appear insignificant in comparison with the advantages which will result.

Action to secure benefits will avoid PROCRASTINATION

IGNORANCE

This may be defined as the failure to understand fully what is being proposed. Sometimes the salesman assumes that the prospect comprehends or appreciates the merits of his proposal, and the pros-

pect's pride may keep him from asking what he thinks are elementary questions.

In such a situation, the salesman should give a clear-cut explanation of the product or service using understandable terms, early in the interview. He should avoid talking in complex technical terminology which the prospect may not understand. He should always be sure that the prospect really understands what he is offering before attempting to obtain a favorable buying decision.

COMPETITION

In selling technical products to industry, the competition may be an outmoded or technically obsolete system or method of measurement. In a truly creative selling effort you may not encounter a human competitor at all. It is very important to determine the presence of this impersonal aspect or form of competition during the early steps to a sale.

We will be concerned only with the conventional interpretation — a rivalry with the representatives and principals who offer similar products and services. Obviously the first step is to identify the competitors who may be involved and then realistically evaluate their proposals and their standing with, or acceptability by, the customer. The salesman should never underrate his competition.

The salesman should learn all he can about his competitor's products and services. To do this he must keep well informed of their newest offerings and of their specific product qualities or features

COMPETITION...

and the related customer benefit claims. This requires alertness in scanning the trade publications, obtaining and studying competitive literature, and observing the products in operation at customers' plants or at trade shows. The salesman should never assume that he knows all that is necessary about his competitors.

His salesmanship manual or warehouse should include a concise listing of the feature-benefit claims as well as the inferior features, or competitive poor qualities which were studied under the selling tools section. The eventual presence of competition should be assumed on most, if not all, selling efforts and discretely phrased competitive comparisons should be made throughout all sales presentations. Wedge questions of the investigation and test variety should be used to determine the specific nature of the competition and the competitor's claims.

There is one form of competition which can be particularly troublesome and this can be termed friendship-competition. This occurs when some influential member of the customer's staff is a close personal friend of the competing salesman. If the presence of such a situation is recognized in time and if the salesman is offering a superior product of value, it is usually possible to overcome this form of competition. It may become necessary to appeal to the biased individual's superior by making a factual presentation of the features, benefits, and economic advantages of the proposal. This should be done as a last resort when the salesman is resigned to the fact that he may never get any of this customer's business. The consequences of appealing to the prospect's supervisor could understandably create ill will which the salesman may never overcome.

In summary, competition must be anticipated, identified, and combatted throughout the sales presentation. Most important, your competition must always be respected; never taken for granted.

63

DIFFICULT PERSONALITY

Can you imagine a prospect who is mean, inconsiderate, arrogant, overbearing, obstinate, and rude—all during the same interview? To be sure, not many prospects fit this description exactly but it is not

uncommon to encounter a few who exhibit a few of these traits during the sales interview. In dealing with this obstacle, it is important to try to determine or understand what causes a person to behave in this manner.

Such things as feelings of insecurity, disappointment, lack of enjoyment of work, illness, or family troubles can turn a normally rational individual into a difficult personality. Whether or not you can interpret the reasons for these moods, the important thing is to remain calm and polite and to overcome any temptation to retaliate by venting your own emotional reactions. Such polite, patient handling of this type of individual will usually pay off. If the cause is superficial, the prospect will regret his ill mannered outburst and assume a more rational attitude.

The salesman should never allow such difficult personality outbursts to divert, block, or permanently interfere with his normal sequence and progress in accomplishing the steps to a sale.

TIME

There are several interpretations of time as an obstacle to making a sale. These all relate to timing and they include:

1. Learning about and starting the selling effort at an early time.
2. Selecting an opportune time for a sales presentation.
3. Appropriate timing in the follow up and closing of a sale.
4. Scheduling and expending sufficient sales call time to penetrate new accounts.

64

The sure way to avoid these time obstacles lies in careful planning in the pre-approach steps to a sale.

A second possible interpretation of time as an obstacle refers to the salesman's personal professional progress. Sales productivity is the product of face-to-face selling time with the prospect multiplied by selling skills. Unless the salesman plans his work to make the most of his time with the prospect and then exercises rigid self discipline in consistently executing such plans, time may become a serious obstacle in his professional progress.

BRUSH-OFF

Perhaps the easiest way to describe this obstacle is to first relate it to consumer selling. Have you ever told a door-to-door salesman or a telephone canvasser, "I'm not interested, I get more magazines than I can possibly read now," or "My insurance program is all set—just reviewed it recently—sorry I'm not in the market now"? If so, you

used a form of brush-off to dismiss the salesman and discourage further solicitation.

The industrial salesman does not encounter this form of brush-off. He is more likely to be told, "Oh, yes, I know all about your products, I will keep you in mind the next time we are in the market." He uses this ruse to obstruct the salesman in the attention or interest steps to a sale because he may not want to spend the time with the salesman, or he may not want to upset his normal buying habits. The beginning salesman may be misled by such tactics. He should never accept such statements at their face value and allow them to divert him from persistently pressing for a sales presentation.

Another form of the brush-off may occur during the desire or decision steps to a sale. Here the prospect may say, "I'm sold on your proposal. I'll take it up with the plant manager and let you know what is decided." This is a buck-passing form of brush-off which also should not be taken at face value. The salesman should politely offer to assist with the preparation and/or presentation of his proposal to the plant manager. Under some circumstances, discretion may dictate accepting this statement for the moment recognizing the need for additional contacts to convince the prospect of the benefits of his proposal. He may later ask for an opportunity to tell his story first hand to the plant manager, if he is really the decision maker.

It is important for the salesman to question such brush-off statements and not allow them to lull him into a false sense of security, thus diverting him from the normal, continuing, decision-getting, follow-up efforts.

Negative Atmosphere

Atmosphere, as a selling tool, embraces those positive, personal, physical, and environmental factors which enhance the sales presentation and the impressions which the prospect receives. Negative

avoid NEGATIVE ATMOSPHERE

atmosphere, as an obstacle, is the opposite of the selling tool, stressing the negative, personal, physical, and environmental factors which obstruct the progress of the sale.

POOR JUDGMENT

This obstacle is the opposite of good judgment as it was defined as a selling tool. Here again, it is repeated in negative form to stress its importance. Poor judgment can be an important contributing factor to

losing an order. Conscientious analysis and objective self-criticism of one's progress in accomplishing the steps to a sale will improve judgment and minimize it as a negative influence.

Suggested Self-Development Exercises

1. Prepare a detailed demonstration procedure for one of your typical products. This may be in outline or written narrative form. It should be sufficiently detailed and complete so that it could be used in a simulated demonstration to a prospect.
2. Write a typical example, based on your own experience, of each of the following obstacles, explaining how you succeeded in overcoming it:

   Habit, Fear, Price, Complaints, Procrastination.
3. Competition.
   A. Study a major product of your principal competitor and make a list of its product qualities and customer benefit claims. Compare this with a product profile of your own corresponding product, using a common profile format.
   B. Make a similar comparison under the headings of prestige, customer acceptance (assurance), and supporting services provided.

67

4. Time.
    A. How do you learn about new sales opportunities? List the various inputs and explain how you time the initial selling effort.
    B. How do you determine the timing for the follow-up sales call and order closing?
5. Brush-off.
    A. Write down several examples of brush-offs that you have encountered.
    B. Explain how you handled them.

Objection Handling Techniques

The surest cure for both obstacles and objections, and they are synonymous, is a carefully planned and well-executed sales presentation which anticipates them by answering them before they are actually stated by the prospect. As a part of this fundamental technique, obstacles are discerned and objections are brought out in the open and disposed of as the sales presentation progresses.

OBJECTION HANDLING TECHNIQUES

The twelve obstacles that comprise all the things which may influence the sale negatively include the objections as well. Fundamental counter-measures have been pointed out. Now we will go beyond the analytical and logic aspects and concentrate on a review of the objection-handling skills which have proven effective in industrial selling.

Objections can be categorized broadly under four headings:
No Need; No Money; No Hurry; No Confidence. If these and similar customer expressions are accepted, the salesman might as well pack up his briefcase and look for more fruitful prospects. Obviously such statements should not be accepted without careful investigation and confirmation of their validity. This leads to the first of six fundamental skills which follow:

1. *Analyze objections carefully*

   Try to determine whether the objection is sincere and valid or whether it is merely an excuse for not buying—a camouflage to conceal more fundamental obstacles like habit or friendship-competition, a deliberate provocation to get you off balance or a stall to dismiss you. Do not take objections at their face value. Consider them as a challenge and an opportunity to emphasize the advantages of your proposal.

2. *Control your temper and never argue*

   Do not consider objections as a personal affront, regardless of the tactless manner in which they may be stated. Maintain your temper and composure and restrain any impulse to disprove your prospect's objection by engaging in an argument. Such tactics will only serve to further irritate him emotionally and they may close the door to you permanently. The prospect may be completely in the wrong, but if so there are more subtle, non-provocative ways of convincing him of this.

3. *Listen, question and listen*

   This technique serves two purposes. The first is that it gives your prospect an opportunity to vent his feelings, without challenge or interruption. This usually has the effect of softening him up and putting him in a more amenable frame of mind. The second purpose is to provide an opportunity for you to learn more about the reasons supporting the objection, to determine its validity, and to decide how best to handle it. Ask brief leading questions to draw the prospect out and learn more about the details which prompted the objection.

4. *Have a sympathetic attitude*

   Make clear your appreciation of the reasons for the prospect's attitude and your sincere desire to eliminate the causes of his objections. In short, show a willingness to admit or concede before you start constructive action to overcome the objection. The prospect will respect you more for patiently and sympathetically listening to him.

5. *Use third party, customer case histories in lieu of objection rebuttals*

   If the prospect's objection is not valid or if it concerns something

69

which has been corrected, the preferred method of communicating the proof of this is to relate the experience of another customer. This involves the use of the story as a selling tool. This technique makes it unnecessary for you to directly dispute or challenge your prospect's contentions. Of greater importance is that it provides an opportunity for your prospect to check directly with a disinterested party. Under certain circumstances involving such things as delivery complaints, it may be necessary to call on an authority in the home office to provide the required assurances against recurrence.

6. *Never allow the objection to divert your sales presentation*
When objections occur during your sales presentation or product demonstration, it may be expedient to divert the objection or to postpone the handling rather than allow it to interrupt the presentation. Simple, straightforward objections may be disposed of immediately. More complex objections may be handled to better advantage with the originator following the presentation. There may be occasions when it will be prudent to delay the handling until a subsequent call at which time you may better answer a complex technical objection.

There are many more ramifications of objection handling situations and techniques. All of these have been covered under the heading Obstacles to a Sale. You have been exposed to the important fundamental causes of objections and to the specific, general purpose objection handling techniques. To acquire skill in using these techniques, it is essential that you conscientiously put them to work in your daily selling activities. Much practice is required to make them really beneficial to you.

In concluding this subject, it should again be emphasized that the surest cure for objections is a carefully planned and well-executed sales presentation which anticipates, and thus hopefully avoids them. You should benefit from your objection handling experiences in planning and composing the next sales presentation.

To clarify this subject further, let's see how a salesman might employ some of the other recommended techniques when faced with a few hypothetical objections which might be raised by his prospect.

Prospect Jones: "So you represent the ABC Recorder Co.? Well, I wouldn't have another one of your recorders in my department if you gave it to me!"

Salesman Smith: "I'm sorry to hear this, sir. Have you had some bad experience in the past?"

Prospect Jones: "I'll say I have. Last year I ordered one of your new circular chart recorders for a rush job. The delivery was so late I had to get another recorder to get the job started."

Salesman Smith: "I can understand your feelings. Did we give any reason for the delay? Was there anything special about the recorder?"

Prospect Jones: "Oh, well, if you call a new chart range special — we had to match a chart which we were already using in that department. Nevertheless, your salesman made the promise with full knowledge of the special chart requirement."

Salesman Smith: "Did the salesman try to help you? It should have been possible to loan you another recorder with a similar range to tide you over until the new chart was ready!"

Prospect Jones: "No, he didn't suggest anything like that. In fact, he was transferred from the territory before the recorder was delivered. Haven't seen anything of him since. Guess I've learned my lesson about dealing with a company that doesn't back me up."

Salesman Smith: "What became of the ABC recorder? Are you using it? Does it work OK?"

Prospect Jones: "Oh, I transferred it to the research lab. They seem to like it fine. It's a good recorder and has some nice features."

Salesman Smith: "Mr. Jones, if you place another order with us, I can assure you this will not happen again. We have a permanent office here now, with a service representative located here also. Furthermore, we make our own charts at the factory now instead of buying them from the outside, and we have better control of shipping promises."

Prospect Jones: "That sounds good, but how do I know I can trust you!"

Salesman Smith: "I'd sure appreciate it if you could take a few minutes to phone these several neighboring plants who have switched to ABC recorders and hear what they have to say about deliveries and back-up service now. You don't have to take my word for it. Then I'd appreciate another opportunity to show you how well our latest recorder performs and how well we can back it up."

The foregoing dialogue illustrates the Listen-question-listen method. When Smith found out the details of the incident which led to the complaint, he was able to point out specific corrective measures which had already been taken and which assured against its repetition. Then he used the selling tool, assurance, to prove his claims by suggesting that Jones check with several other local users. He also displayed a sympathetic attitude throughout the discussion.

Let's try one more example of the handling of a typical complaint.

Prospect Jones: "That was an interesting demonstration, Smith, your new recorder has some good features all right, but your price is too high. Your competition is about 20% lower in price and I don't see how I can justify such a big difference to my management!"

Salesman Smith: "I can appreciate how you feel, Mr. Jones, and the initial cost of our recorder is higher. Your recorder performance requirements are quite critical, however, and it could be that this initial price difference might be recovered after you use the recorder for a while. You know Tom Brown, over at the National Missile Test Site, I believe. His recorder applications are similar to yours. He, too, was concerned about the initial cost difference when he put in that new installation last year. Tom told me recently that he already has saved more than that extra cost, because the ABC high speed features permit him to record more channels on each chart, reducing the number of recorders required per test unit. A further saving is gained because the pressurized inking feature, with resulting bold, legible record, makes it possible to quickly reproduce or duplicate chart records with existing direct copy machines. This is in contrast to the slower, more costly copy methods which the other type chart records require. Because of the built-in reliability of the ABC recorder Tom is making additional savings in maintenance and reduced down-time. I'd appreciate it if you would check with him before making a decision. It's very likely that his cost saving experience would be sufficient to support your requisition for ABC recorders"

Here the salesman used a third party, customer case history story, to overcome what appeared to be a formidable price obstacle. This was much more effective than a generalized rebuttal consisting of theoretical product quality, customer benefit claims. Smith had a very convincing case history story, of course. Quite often an unfavorable price differential can be justified by similar stories illustrating the plus services which you and your company render.

Suggested Self-Development Exercises
1. Make a list of as many different type objections that you can remember that have occurred in recent months.
2. Write what you would say in answer to:
   A. Your price is too high.
   B. We're standardized on brand X. It would be too costly to switch now.

C. Our present method is good enough — we don't need anything better.

D. We experienced some bad quality problems with your equipment last year. I'm afraid my project engineers will not specify them again.

3. Based on your own experience, what are the three most frequently stated objections?

Order Closing Techniques

Closing the order does not usually comprise a deliberate act, involving some novel technique, which is performed near the end of the interview. The accomplished salesman designs his sales presentation in such a manner that asking for an order may be the logical climax. As he progresses through the interest and desire steps to the

ORDER CLOSING TECHNIQUES

sale, he observes his prospect's reactions carefully and he uses wedge questions of the test and suggestion types to try to determine which of his sales tools, i.e. product quality, customer benefit, loss, service, has the greatest impact. He also uses good judgement to interpret these several prospect impressions to determine the practicability of asking for an order at any time during the interview.

The normal order closing strategy is to summarize the strong points of his proposal — based on observations made during the sales presentation — and then to ask for the order in a straightforward manner. Being timid and fearful of rejection may inhibit the beginning salesman from making such a direct request. If so, he should realize that in most cases the prospect expects some kind of order closing attempt. These strong points or key issues usually include the most significant product quality, and customer benefit claims. Impressive loss points in the form of stories giving additional proof of the benefit claims may also stimulate a favorable purchasing decision.

Another commonly used tactic is to offer as a further inducement such things as a minor price concession, a preferred delivery schedule, or free installation supervision or start-up service, if the order is placed immediately.

The important thing is to climax each sales presentation and product demonstration with some form of order closing or purchasing decision commitment effort. The minimum objective should be an agreement to have the prospect evaluate the merits of the proposal further and to make a date for a return visit, thus keeping the door open. The salesman should not be discouraged by the prospect's refusal to make a positive commitment on his first or second order closing attempt. Accomplishing a creative sale usually requires persistent follow up and at least several order closing attempts.

Before leaving the subject of salesmanship, some time will be devoted to the development of a selling formula which is an easy-to-remember paraphrase of the previously covered, detailed, steps to a sale.

The Selling Formula

HOW + WHAT + WHY + WHO = THE ORDER

The formula is readily applicable to the typical sales presentation and its purpose is to remind you of the selling tools which have proven most effective in accomplishing these four steps to a sale.

Here's *how* to get attention and interest on a prospecting type of sales call. Use tools: atmosphere (personal and environmental); prestige (personal and company); pride; service; contact; and wedge questions.

This sequence is typical but not mandatory, but all six tools are appropriate, and a creative sales call should include them.

Then tell the prospect *what* you can do for him, thus creating a desire for your products. Use tools: customer benefits, assurance and story.

74

SELLING FORMULA

$$A^1 B^2 V_1 = \text{THE ORDER}$$

Then show him *why* you can do as you claim and do it better than your competitors, thus strengthening his desire and paving the way for a more favorable decision. Use tools: product qualities (always with reference to resulting customer benefits), competitive poor qualities, loss, prestige and service.

Finally, point out *who* uses your products and enjoys the benefits

P-D-P Selling Formula To Get *PLUS* Business

First—Here's

HOW to get attention and interest on a missionary sales call

+ Use Tools: 11-5-6-9-10-12

Tell Prospect

WHAT you can do for him — thus creating a desire for your product

+ Use Tools: 1-7-8

Show

WHY you can do as you claim — and do it better than your competitors

+ Use Tools: 2-3-4-5-9

Point Out

WHO uses your products and enjoys the benefits you have claimed

Use Tools: 7-8-1-13

Then all you have to do is ask for **= THE ORDER**

SALES TOOLS
USE THEM WISELY

1. Customer Benefits	6. Pride
2. Product Qualities	7. Assurance
	8. Story
3. Competitive Poor Qualities	9. Service
4. Loss Points	10. Contact
5. Prestige	11. Atmosphere
	12. Wedge Questions
13. Good Judgement	

TO OVERCOME THESE
OBSTACLES

1. Habit	8. Difficult Personality
2. Fear	9. Time
3. Price	10. Brush-Off
4. Complaints	11. Negative Atmosphere
5. Procrastination	
6. Ignorance	12. Poor Judgement
7. Competition	

you have claimed. Use tools: assurance, story, customer benefits and good judgement.

All that remains is to ask for the order.

THE ORDER

Another simple way of describing the selling formula is shown in the accompanying illustration, which is a wallet-size card that lists the sales tools and the obstacles on one side and the selling formula on the other side. A similar card can be made by the salesman for ready reference and review of the selling fundamentals which he can look over while he is in the reception room waiting to see his prospect. This little card can be an invaluable reminder of a selling tool to stress or it may alert you to an obstacle which should be explored and overcome.

Part 3

Marketing and Management in the Sales Territory

Introductory Comments

Marketing and management play a major role in the field sales territory as well as in the home office. While these functions are relatively passive in nature when compared to face-to-face salesmanship, they represent the research, planning, and control required to maximize the salesman's productivity and his important contributions to the company's overall sales growth.

Sales Territory Analysis and Planning

Sales territory analysis and planning are an indispensable requirement from the salesman's point of view. Without a thorough understanding of what his assigned area includes in terms of active customers, prospective customers, and unidentified or suspect

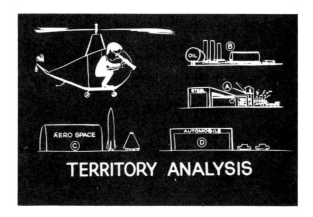

companies, he cannot intelligently plan his daily work. To do an effective job of work planning he must also establish a relative degree of importance to these companies and he should make a realistic estimate of the time required to cover them adequately. Such a basic analysis should be made in depth initially, and it should be updated at least annually. When completed, the analysis provides a realistic basis from which to plan how the limited field coverage time at his disposal may be utilized most effectively to insure maximum sales yield and optimum earnings from his territory.

This subject is equally important to the district sales supervisor and to his management. Lacking such fundamental knowledge, it is difficult, if not impossible, to staff the field offices intelligently and to anticipate field personnel requirements to match sales growth. Sales territory analysis and forward planning can be the key to accelerated sales growth, increased corporate profits and higher earnings for the salesman. It is an important sales management function which many companies fail to perform realistically. Some companies rely entirely on their home office sales records and history, assuming continuation of the status quo, and make no effort to reappraise or update their sales territory intelligence periodically.

Sales territory analysis and planning is important because:

1. It provides a valid measurement of the total sales potential for the company's specific products.
2. It gives a realistic estimate of the degree of penetration in the company's markets.
3. It provides essential market intelligence on which to base present sales manpower requirements and sound future planning.
4. It can be a useful tool in providing more reliable and realistic sales forecasts.
5. It is an indispensable tool for intelligent field sales coverage and daily work planning and control.

The task of territory analysis and planning should be a joint responsibility of the salesman and his district manager and it requires their close cooperation to accomplish it effectively. The procedures outlined represent the experience and conclusions resulting from an in-depth study performed by the author in cooperation with a large multi-division manufacturer of sophisticated technical products. This study was conducted first on a test basis in one large regional sales area. Based on this experience, formats and procedures were developed and the project was expanded into a nation-wide effort. As a result of this comprehensive analysis there was considerable relocation of salesmen to match the potential business distribution, there were additions to sales manpower to permit more aggressive effort to invade areas where the competition was dominant and there was the inception of specialized-by-product selling in certain areas where government sponsored business was abundant and highly concentrated. In other words, the forms and procedures suggested are the result of considerable investigation and experience and they are applicable to all companies that sell and market technically oriented products to the industrial and government markets.

CUSTOMER: _____   CUSTOMER WORK SHEET

LOCATION: _____   SALES IN $1,000

KIND OF BUSINESS: _____

DATE: _____

BUYING POTENTIAL CATEGORY: A__ B__ C__ D__

PRODUCTS	COMPANY	COMPETITION	19__ POTENTIAL	COVERAGE MAN-DAYS
Product I				
Actual 1969	_____	_____		
Est. 1970	_____	_____		
Est. 1971	_____	_____		
Average	_____	_____	_____	_____
Product II				
Actual 1969	_____	_____		
Est. 1970	_____	_____		
Est. 1971	_____	_____		
Average	_____	_____	_____	_____
Product III				
Actual 1969	_____	_____		
Est. 1970	_____	_____		
Est. 1971	_____	_____		
Average	_____	_____	_____	_____
Product IV				
Actual 1969	_____	_____		
Est. 1970	_____	_____		
Est. 1971	_____	_____		
Average	_____	_____	_____	_____
Total Average	_____	_____	_____	_____

Comments:

DIST. _____ F.E. _____

Using a form similar to the customer work sheet for each customer of record and each prospective customer, the following is an outline of the recommended procedure in making an initial territory analysis:

1. Tabulate the customers of record, listing the following information:
   A. Company name and corporate affiliation.
   B. Location: city, county, state.
   C. Kind of business: manufacturer—by industry category—original equipment manufacturer—government (department and facility)—institution (educational, research)—contracting engineer and distributor-dealer.
   D. Company sales by product category and dollar sales volume.
   E. Competitors' sales by product category and dollar sales volume.
   F. Estimate of sales coverage time required in man-days per year. This should include travel time to and from the company's location.
2. Tabulate the competitors' accounts and other prospect and suspect accounts, listing as much of the above data as practical. Make an estimate of the customer's sales if this cannot be obtained directly. To obtain these prospect names, review all reference sources including state and county manufacturer directories, trade association directories, government publications—standard industrial code directory, other local sources.

Summarize these individual customer work sheets by sales territory on a form similar to the territory analysis summary sheet.

The next steps in the utilization of this initial analysis data are as follows:

1. Categorize all accounts according to their annual buying potential
   A. Over $50,000.
   B. Between $10,000 and $50,000.
   C. Under $10,000.
   D. Prospect or suspect—potential sales unknown.
2. Summarize all accounts by these categories, identifying their purchasing potential as to A, B, C, or D. Group the accounts of record. The competitive accounts and the prospect or suspect accounts should be grouped under separate headings.
3. Determine the average man-days per year coverage time requirement for each account category A, B, C, and D. In the suspect category assume the time requirement of 10% of the total of the other two categories (accounts of record and competitive accounts). This assumes that 10% of the available coverage time will be devoted to prospecting calls.

TERRITORY ANALYSIS SUMMARY SHEET
(SALES IN $1,000)

Region _____
District _____
Date _____

Customer Location Kind of Business	PRODUCT I				PRODUCT II				(Etc.)	TOTALS ALL PRODUCTS			
	Company	Competition	Total	Man Days	Company	Competition	Total	Man Days		Company	Competition	Total	Man Days
TOTALS													

4. Tabulate for the accounts of record and for the competitive accounts, the total sales potential in thousands of dollars per year; and the estimated sales coverage time in man-days per year.
5. Using an average of 170 man-days per year per man, compute the theoretical manpower requirements in the territory. This is done by dividing the estimated total coverage time by 170. This 170 man-day figure was derived earlier, assuming approximately 75% of the 220 days available for selling is spent in travel and face-to-face contact with the prospect.
6. Compare this with the existing manpower total. If the existing manpower is insufficient, determine the amount of personnel expansion which can be economically justified. Hire and train the additional manpower.
7. Work out a total territory coverage plan including selective selling campaigns and an allowance for some prospect and some suspect investigation calls.
8. In cooperation with the salesman, work out individual territory coverage plans with a tentative schedule sheet for the A and B account categories.
9. Devise a simple call report system (with a quarterly summary report feature) to check the accomplishment of the work plan. This should be used in conjunction with a quarterly report of sales by territories by customers in order to measure actual sales progress.
10. Review, refine and, if necessary, revise the territory analysis and coverage plans every six months.

It was pointed out earlier that the successful accomplishment of this territory analysis and planning task will benefit the salesman, the district manager, the regional manager, and the company and home office management. The following is a summary of specific benefits which will result from the successful accomplishment and application of these analyses:

1. Permits accurate determination of sales manpower requirements.
2. Points up the need for specialized selling effort by either product or market categories.
3. Provides the salesman with a sound basis on which to determine his daily, weekly, and long range territory work plans and objectives.
4. Makes possible maximum sales call productivity and effectiveness with accompanying optimum earnings for the salesman.
5. Stimulates the development of selective and creative selling campaigns.

6. Provides the salesman and the district manager with experience in a most important sales management function.

In concluding this subject, it is strongly recommended that both the salesman and his management cooperatively undertake this suggested sales territory analysis and territory sales coverage planning study. Ideally it should be a nation-wide effort. If there is some question regarding the specific procedures and formats they may have to be custom-designed for the company's business or products. A sample or test study should be conducted in one area to obtain the experience required to modify the suggested formats and the basic parameters used for determining manpower coverage.

Selling to the Government Markets

Selling to the government markets entails some special strategies and skills, many of which are acquired by experience. These strategies will vary according to the nature of the products and also

SELLING GOVERNMENT MARKETS

the dollar value of the procurement. They may vary also depending on the point of purchase; i.e., a government institution, agency or facility, prime contractor or sub-contractor. Occasionally, the major purchasing influence is exercised at some agency remote from the point of purchase, which may be a prime contractor. It would not be practical to attempt to cover in this chapter the special strategies applicable to the more complex government procurement cycles.

This can be done more effectively by your field sales manager with specific reference to your own products and to the government procurement channels normally employed.

Please do not infer from the foregoing that selling to the government markets is a highly specialized art requiring skills and strategies which are inscrutable. This is not so. All of the fundamentals of salesmanship and the skills in applying them which have been studied in the earlier text are applicable and pertinent to the entire gamut of government market exploitation and selling. The government procurement cycles and procedures may be more complicated than those in a typical industrial market procurement, but the same opportunities to influence the product specifications and the purchasing decision favorably are almost always present somewhere within the procurement circuit. The fundamental techniques employed to create these favorable influences are identical with those studied earlier.

Government procurements may be categorized broadly under two headings: non-negotiable, and negotiable. The non-negotiable procurement method most commonly employed is the I.F.B. or the Invitation For Bids. This invitation describes the products or services required in finite terms which include complete specifications and/or brand and model number identification. The basic intent of this form of procurement is to obtain at least several responsive or qualifying quotations. The order or contract is then awarded to the bidder offering the lowest price. While there may be some question about the low bidder's ability to satisfy the specifications fully, there is no opportunity for price negotiation.

Usually the salesman cannot influence the type of bid form. If it is subject to influence, however, and if the salesman can create a strong preference for his company's products, it is normally desirable to press for the I.F.B. form of procurement. He may then have the opportunity to assist in the preparation of the I.F.B. product description and performance specifications. If this is done skillfully, with emphasis on those good qualities or standard features of his products which his competitors cannot economically match, he is almost certain to receive the contract award. His competitors may protest the award based on discrimination but this involves too much risk, for the legality aspect is usually a question of interpretation and the protest may be reviewed by persons who are not technically qualified to make sound judgments. Such protests are risky since they may reflect on the integrity of the procurement personnel with a resulting alienation of future relationships with the protesting bidder. Another successful technique which may be employed in writing I.F.B. specifications is to deliberately use some of the product terminology (i.e. feature name) of the major competitor. The purpose of this is to make the invitation appear to be innocuous, thus disarming the competition into quoting a higher price. About 50 percent of the I.F.B. specifications based on a specific product brand name will permit several responsive bids. The other 50 percent are written with the deliberate intent to exclude competition. Assuming the salesman can influence the specifications, the technique to be employed will depend on the conditions or circumstances surrounding this particular procurement.

The negotiable procurement category includes the following:

1. The R.F.P. - Request For Proposal
2. R.F.Q. - Request For Quotation
3. The Negotiated Contract.

All of these procurement forms leave room for variation of the specifications. Their purpose is to get recommendations from the vendors. In effect, the procuring agency is soliciting ideas as well as price estimates. It is seldom that the salesman has any opportunity to influence the form in which a negotiable procurement is issued. If he should have this opportunity the R.F.P. form is desirable because it gives the buyer considerable latitude in making the award, regardless of price considerations.

The R.F.P. method is quite similar to selling to the industrial markets and identical selling techniques may be employed to influence the specifier and the buyer. If the favored salesman's bid is not the lowest, he must then reassure the buyer by convincing him of the superiority of his products, thus allaying the buyer's fear of criticism for paying the higher price. The R.F.P. is the most commonly employed negotiable procurement form. It usually gives a loose description of the material or services required.

As a general rule, the supervisory government procurement people prefer the I.F.B. procurement method because it invites competition with resulting lower prices. The local government facility people frequently prefer the R.F.P. method because it offers a better opportunity to get the materials or services which they prefer.

Communications in the Field

The salesman and his field office supervisor are the most important source of customer and market intelligence, intelligence which is vital if not indispensable to his management for the guidance of his

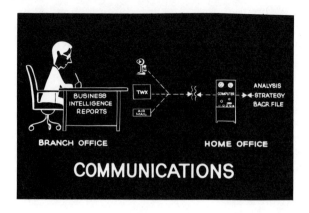

COMMUNICATIONS

company. A wide variety of information is needed by the salesman and by his management and the problem of recording and communicating this information is both difficult and complex. Too often the salesman and his supervisor are burdened with comprehensive and detailed reporting procedures, which if carried out literally would seriously cut into their effective, face-to-face customer selling time. Usually such comprehensive, time consuming reporting systems do not accomplish their theoretical objectives and fall of their own weight. Because of their impracticability and dubious value the salesman's compliance is usually done in a perfunctory manner. More often the systems fall into disuse with the result that essential field intelligence is not communicated to management on a regular basis.

Fortunately, there is a practical solution to this communications problem. A review of all of the typical information input categories should be made. The truly worthy ones should be identified and suggestions for streamlined reporting procedures should be made. This section will be concerned with both the field and the home office aspects of the problem. Before going into them, we will digress briefly to review some of the fundamentals of composing and writing letters and reports which serve the more general purpose of local sales promotion, and communications of routine nature which do not comprise reporting procedures.

Sales Letter and Report Writing

Writing sales letters, memoranda and reports in the field offices appears to have become somewhat of a lost art in this era of high speed, low cost, communication methods. The advent of direct dial, long distance, credit card-reimbursed telephone service, data-phone, and TWX systems has resulted in a reduction in both the quantity and quality of the sales letters and memoranda written by the field salesman. It seems much easier for the salesman to drive out to see his customer or to telephone him under many circumstances where a letter could serve the purpose to equal, or better, advantage.

Sales letters written in the field usually serve one of three broad purposes:

1. The routine transmittal of information relating to the order details, delivery information, service matters and confirmation of oral agreements.
2. Local sales promotion where the letter may serve as a supplementary sales contact, in between regular sales calls. Such letters may inquire about current requirements and suggest a call in person on a contemplated trip to this vicinity. Of greatest value is the local direct-mail method of quickly disseminating, on a personalized, selective basis, pertinent new product information, application stories and bulletins, trade show invitations, and the like. With modern automated typing methods, such letters can be produced in quantity with personalized salutations, at moderate cost. There is plenty of opportunity in this category for innovation by the enterprising salesman.
3. Follow-up of a sales presentation or proposal. Most rewarding as far as sales are concerned, is the use of a letter to follow up a recent sales presentation or a product demonstration. This provides an opportunity to thank the prospect for the demonstration opportunity and for the courtesies extended by his staff. It should also contain a brief reminder or confirmation of the most significant sales advantages. A succinct summary of the product quality, customer benefit claims, loss examples, assurance points in the form of selected references, and service benefits is appropriate for this purpose. This is best done in outline form. The letter may also contain important points which may have been overlooked during the interview. It is usually addressed to the several individuals who witnessed the presentation and who may influence the purchasing decision. Appropriate literature may be included also.

These types of letters are not difficult to write. They should be written in an informal, conversational manner. Clichés and stereotyped expressions should be avoided as should the frequent use of the word "I." Short sentences, and simple, easily understood language should be used.

The degree of formality in the salutation of the letter should of course depend on the extent of familiarity that the salesman has with his prospect or customer. When in doubt, use a conservative, more formal approach. Be careful to spell the prospect's name and to list his title accurately.

The purpose of the letter should be stated briefly in the opening paragraph. The body of the letter should use short paragraphs and an outline format where appropriate. The concluding paragraph should suggest the desired action, which may be to arrange an appointment for a sales presentation or a product demonstration. The conclusion may constitute a straightforward attempt to get favorable action or an order closing decision.

As a communication tool, the memorandum to the home office can be a supplement and sometimes a preferred substitute for a long distance telephone call. The time saving advantages can be substantial, providing more time for productive face-to-face selling contact. Frequently, a memorandum conveying the request or outlining the problem is mailed in advance of a scheduled telephone call, permitting the home office to obtain this information in anticipation of the call. Complex information and data can be transmitted more completely and accurately and, through multiple copies, more people can be informed with minimum time expenditure.

The technique in writing memoranda is basically the same as that used in report writing. Most of the fundamentals described earlier are applicable. The purpose is always stated first. If the report is lengthy it may be desirable to include also a brief synopsis of the findings in the introductory paragraphs. This is followed by a detailed description of the problem and the methods which were employed to implement and solve it. The conclusion should contain the findings and recommendations with a clearly stated request for the action to carry them out.

Sales letter and memorandum writing should not be considered an essential chore. When carefully planned and written, such communications can serve as a valuable selling adjunct when dealing with a prospect or with the home office. As the salesman moves up into supervisory and marketing functions, he will be required to write more reports. His demonstrated capabilities in writing letters and reports while in the field can be a significant factor in the rate at which he moves upward in the selling and marketing profession.

Field Sales Reporting Practices

Before getting into the specifics of reporting procedures, let's review some of the typical purposes for which reports are usually required.

1. Territory sales coverage
   Recording calls on customers and prospects noting routine information including the date, purpose of the call, and the name of the individual contacted. These may be individual or summary reports and they should make provision for noting personnel changes and mailing list category validation, corrections and additions.
2. Local sales control
   The reports should provide the basis for a periodic summary of the salesman's customer contacts. They should also require a week-in-advance written plan of the customer calls to be made during that week. This will insure a minimal basis for the salesman and his supervisor to review his plans versus his performance.
3. Business activity reports
   The simplest form in this category would merely report on the current status or the final disposition of routine, outstanding quotations of average value. A more specific requirement would entail status reports of large proposals, bids, or negotiations. Such individual reports should include current status, important recent developments, competitive situations and the final disposition of the quotation. These reports would keep the home office advised of the status of the proposal at regular intervals.
4. Business outlook
   New business opportunities comprising plant expansions or new plant construction. Short and long range business forecasts. Territory analysis and sales potential by accounts.
5. Product performance reports
   These should include feedback of significant customer complaints or comments relative to accuracy, reliability, service ability.
6. Suggestions for new products or product improvements
   These may result from the salesman's personal observations or from suggestions made by user companies.
7. Competitive product information and sales intelligence
   Includes all unusual competitive activities.

CRITERIA FOR REPORTS

To insure the propriety and necessity of field sales reports and also their effective utilization, the following considerations should be kept in mind. First, the reports must have recognizable value to the salesman, to his field supervisors and to his home-office marketing management.

Second, they should make a minimum demand on the salesman's time and his supervisor's time, which should be in proportion to the value of the reports. To be effective the reports must be mandatory and they must be submitted punctually. This applies to both the initial reporting phase as well as to the information utilization and feedback phases. Significant reports should be monitored continually in the field and the home office.

BUSINESS ACTIVITY CONTACT REPORTS

There is a definite need for an individual sales contact reporting system which will serve a constructive purpose for the salesman and his supervisor and which will provide direct communication of business intelligence to the home office marketing groups.

The salesman needs a simple, convenient form for recording results of his contacts with his customers. When selling complex technical products, it is not practical to depend on memory or on fragmentary notes for follow-up calls, project status reports, recording customer personnel changes, and for special home office requests.

The typical salesman carries too much essential information in his head or in his pocket notebook instead of in the district office files. Vital information may be lost when a salesman leaves the company or is transferred to another territory. The sales contact report form should be designed to provide maximum usefulness for the salesman. Conversely, it should not be designed as a multi-purpose form to serve as a supervisory control tool, a market research input means, an accounting device or a host of other purposes which many forms try to serve.

For the sales supervisor, it should provide a permanent record of significant customer contacts. It may be used to review the salesman's activities when there is some question about his productivity. It may also be used to update business activity reports and to post progress in the development of business obtained from key prospects and customers. These are but a few of the practical uses which the supervisor can make of sales contact reports.

The home office marketing groups can also benefit from such sales contact reports. Copies of all reports should be sent to the home office where they can serve a variety of worthwhile uses. All reports involving quotation status changes would be scanned and the changed data would be extracted and used to update a business activities summary report which will be described later in the text. Information about important new programs and new business opportunities or any special request would be referred, by means of a signal on the contact report, to the market or product manager involved. When there are important changes in customer personnel, the advertising department would be alerted to cross check mailing list records and make the necessary changes or additions.

This form is sometimes referred to as a business activity contact report and it should be filled out by the salesman following each customer contact—personal call or a significant telephone contact—

BUSINESS ACTIVITY CONTACT REPORTS

to report a prospective business opportunity or a significant development or change in status of an existing program, project or proposal. It should be used to report progress in the development of key customers and prospects as identified by the territory analysis and evaluation procedure described earlier. Its use should be mandatory by all salesmen for all contacts.

SALES CONTACT REPORT

Customer
Name _____ | DO | Sequence # | G/M/I | FE | Account # |

↳ Write a "Q" here if a formal quotation

Address _____ has been made. --- Fill in address,
City & city and state on first report only.
State _____ Home office will look up customer
account number.

Quantity Type Number Amount

E	___ ___ ___)		(Month Percent	P
Q	___ ___ ___)		(	R
U	___ ___ ___)	Total	(——— ———	O
I	___ ___ ___)	Total Probability	(___ ___	B
P	___ ___ ___)	Amount of order	(——— ———	A
M	___ ___ ___)		(——— ———	B
E	___ ___ ___) $ ___ ___%	(___ ___	I
N	___ ___ ___)		(	L
T	___ ___ ___)		(Beyond ___	I
	___ ___ ___)		(	T
				Y

BAR Comments: _____

| Program Name | Has funding been approved? ☐ yes ☐ no | Competitive Probability % | Contact Date |

Other Comments: _____
_____
_____
_____

Name and Title of key people and persons interviewed:
1. _____ 2. _____
3. _____ 4. _____

Routing - Marketing Administration
            Product Marketing Mgr. _____ By _____
            _____ _____ Date _____
            _____ _____

The first example of a business activity contact report is typical of the current report form being used for this purpose. It comprises a set of three padded IBM-size cards. The original top copy is sent to the home office in the special envelope provided which is directed to a marketing administrative services group that processes and/or forwards them to designated individuals. No one person is expected to read all the contact reports. Many reports are simply processed for extraction and posting of project status changes and would not be passed along for individual attention. One carbon copy is retained by the salesman, possibly to be carried in his car in a small file box for convenient reference. The second carbon copy is for the district office where it is filed alphabetically by salesman's territory following any local processing which might be required. Examples of such processing include local updating of a business activity summary report, and posting in a key account profile which would be mandatory.

Typical data that this form might include: salesman and territory numbers; customer name, number, location, individuals visited; market code, program or project name, quotation number and type; company product code, equipment quantity, price; competitive equipment, quantity, price; month of capture, % capture, value x % capture; and trigger code for drop, I.F.B., L.B.R., refer to market manager, product manager, advertising. If computer processing services are available the bottom of the card should be coded for this purpose. This first example shows such a coding.

The other side of the report may be used for pertinent comments, special requests, home office information regarding sales obstacles or new business prospects which require home office action. It may also serve as a lost business report although a separate L.B.R. form is preferable. The primary purpose of the front of the form is to provide information to record the sales call and to update projects listed on the business activity report summary.

BUSINESS ACTIVITY REPORT SUMMARY

The specific design of this summary report must be influenced by the manufacturing company's pertinent products, markets and planning procedures. The typical format which is shown here may be modified to match the company's specific needs. Initial entries on this summary form may be made from quotation copies or from the business activity contact reports in certain situations. Status changes would be posted by the marketing administrative services group utilizing data from the reports. The summary is normally issued semi-monthly by sales territory and it is distributed to the designated field and home office personnel. The district office copies may be posted in the intervening weeks in the field offices utilizing the office copies of the report. The alternate week local updating of the summaries would contribute to the practice of conducting weekly reviews with the salesman.

WEEKLY SUMMARY REPORT OF SALES CALLS PLANNED AND SALES CALLS MADE

This form is for use in the field exclusively and no copies go elsewhere. It serves two important purposes. The first and most important is to encourage the salesman to plan his week's work and

BUSINESS ACTIVITY REPORT SUMMARY

Total Identified Opportunities $
Total Outstanding Quotations

Identified Market Potential $
Statistical Potential
Plant Forecast

Date	Customer/Opportunity Information	Equipment		Amount	Probability		Comments
		Quantity	Type		Total	Mo.	

time utilization in advance. It will reflect in some measure his longer range business development and key prospect cultivation plans resulting from his latest territory analysis and account evaluation. The second purpose is as a supervisory tool. It provides the district manager with a quick look at each salesman's work plan versus accomplishment, and it can be used to advantage during periodic conferences with his men. Many companies use some form of this call plan, and it has demonstrated thoroughly its effectiveness as a local supervisory tool.

RESUME OF LAST WEEK'S ACTIVITIES

REPORT OF		FOR WEEK ENDING	196
Date Visited	Name and Location of Customer or Prospect	Resume of Results	Date of Next Call

COMMENTS:

Give Proposal Number and/or Acknowledgement Number where applicable.

Date	City and State	Hotel	Will call on	P	C	S	I

ITINERARY OF   FOR WEEK ENDING   19

Comments:

P - Prospect

C - Customer   Signed _____

S - Service call

I - Installation Call   Today's Date _____ 196__

Prepare and mail each Saturday:

One copy to Marketing Manager, Instr. Div.
One copy to Regional Sales Manager
Retain one copy for your files

Lost Business Report

Many companies require the salesman to fill out and submit to his supervisor a report of all orders lost. A typical example of one of the simpler formats used is shown. The data requested and the time required to fill out the report are not excessive. It is not unusual to accumulate substantial expense in time, travel, and other costs when attempting to sell a large job. The additional chore of reporting these significant factors which contributed to the loss of the sale can be minor compared with the benefits which may be gained from a review of this experience.

LOST BUSINESS REPORT

District Office: _____   Register No.: _____   Report No.: _____

Date Bus. Placed _____   Date of Report: _____

A. CUSTOMER: _____   Phone: _____

Address: _____

Facility or Dept: _____

Names and Location of Cust. Personnel: _____

_____

_____

B. PRODUCTS INVOLVED: _____

_____

_____

_____

_____ Our Quoted Price: _____

C. ORDER WENT TO: _____ Purchase Price: _____

Your reasons business was lost (in order of importance).

1. _____

2. _____

3. _____

4. _____

Comments: _____

_____

_____

REGIONAL MANAGER'S EVALUATION

Number in order of Importance	Comments:
_____ Price	_____
_____ Delivery	_____
_____ Quality	_____
_____ Applicability	_____
_____ Coverage	_____
_____ Salesmanship	_____

By: _____   Regional Manager

Submitted by: _____

MARKETING DIRECTOR (via regional mgr.)

To be useful, lost business reports should not degenerate into alibi sheets. They should be required only where there were important factors of which both the local and home office management should be apprised. The loss of smaller, run of the mill quotations may be reported on the business activity contact report described earlier. The lost business report should always be reviewed by the district or regional manager who may wish to add supplementary comments before forwarding them to the home office.

KEY ACCOUNT PROFILE

Customer Name _____ Account Number _____

Address _____ City & State _____

Phone_____ TWX _____ Telex _____

In the following section briefly describe customer history and type of products. Maintain a summary of contacts showing date, Field Engineer name and describe results of call.

_____

_____

_____

_____

_____

_____

_____

_____

_____

_____

_____

_____

_____

_____

_____

KEY PERSONNEL			
Name	Title/Department	Date	Remarks

SUMMARY OF EQUIPMENT			
Manufacturer/Model	Date Acquired	Manufacturer/Model	Date Acquired

KEY ACCOUNT PROFILE

This provides a means for recording, in permanent form, all essential information concerning each important customer and prospect. This master record, which should never be removed from the district office, may be initiated from a territory analysis and account evaluation. It should be updated by subsequent periodic analysis and it should contain quarterly and annual postings of shipments by product code. It is desirable to post sales quarterly, taking the data from the business activity summary report.

These master records should be 8-1/2″ by 11″ bond paper with headings for the vital statistics, including the names of influential personnel, business placed, competitive business estimates, sales coverage objectives and sales calls made—all on a quarterly entry basis.

Supervisory Responsibilities Shared by the Salesman

The degree of success attained by any sales and marketing organization is determined in large part by the capability of its individual members. The leadership and continuous motivation of the selling and marketing staff are an equally important factor. Both are vital to

SELECTION OF SALESMEN

achieve maximum sales productivity and a sales growth rate which assures profits and earnings to justify the investment of the company and its share holders. The sales and marketing chief carries much of this tremendous responsibility and he leans heavily on his marketing and selling staffs to play their part in discharging this responsibility. Therefore, the selection of salesmen is highly important.

Unfortunately, all of the factors influencing the selection of sales and marketing personnel cannot be precisely measured, and considerable skill and experience are required to make sound hiring judgments.

There are interviewing and testing methods available which can be scored in some measure, thus assisting the supervisor in making the hiring decisions. Most of these tests can be categorized as one of the following types: intelligence or mental ability, vocational interests, personality traits, vocabulary capability, mechanical and other specific abilities, and aptitude tests relating specifically to the job requirements. Most of these tests have proven to be fairly reliable, positive aids to making the selection decision. Conversely, they can quickly point out weaknesses which should disqualify the applicant. Other tests relating to various forms of aptitude identification are much less reliable.

There are several basic reasons why aptitude tests for salesmen are so often failures. Interpretation can be faulty. An interest in football does not make a man a good player. Neither does an interest in selling make him a potential salesman. The applicant may fake the answers if he desires. The average applicant can easily see through what is sought in an aptitude test and provide the right answers. Perhaps the most condemning reason is that specific aptitude tests have a tendency to seek conformity which results in average people with average capabilities. Most tests tend to screen out the imaginative, the impulsive, the original, the aggressive individual—the man who might really make a top salesman.

Research indicates that two central characteristics are essential to successful selling. One is empathy, and the second is a certain ego drive, an inner hunger to persuade and convince in an intensely personal way. These are even more important in a salesman than experience, which, all too often, is simply experience in being mediocre.

Test scores can be misleading if the motivation to utilize apparent capabilities is lacking. Another truth is that good supervision, which includes the ability to recognize accomplishment, provide guidance, to motivate and to inspire, can bring out and exploit the latent capabilities displayed by the applicant when the hiring decision was made. Suggestions and examples of successful techniques will be given under the heading of "Supervisory and Performance Review Practices."

The Selection Procedure

Selecting a salesman can be difficult, particularly when applicants have had no previous selling experience and sometimes, as in the case of a recent college graduate, no work record of any kind. It is most difficult to assess and predict the presence and the extent of certain personality traits such as: industriousness or drive, self discipline or the willingness and ability to work independently, persistence and persuasiveness, enthusiasm and the ability to take reverses without being demoralized.

The risks in selecting applicants with previous selling experience are somewhat less because of the reference checking opportunity. In this latter situation there may still be hazards. When a capable, experienced salesman changes jobs there are things which may not be known from the reference checks. What caused the applicant to seek a new job? That there was dissatisfaction is evident but was it really on the part of the individual? Quite often it can be traced to the employer who recognizes the weakness or other limitations of the man and is happy to see him leave. When queried as a reference, some supervisors accentuate the positive qualities and are reluctant to divulge the real basis for their dissatisfaction.

In building or expanding a selling organization, it may be preferable to do it the hard way — select men who possess the desired qualifications and have some demonstrated work record other than selling, and then carefully train them. Hiring, indoctrinating, and training a salesman usually costs upward of $10,000 regardless of how much or how little selling experience he may have at the time of hiring.

The selection procedure varies in complexity according to the size of the company and its selling and marketing staff. In its early stage, the typical small company cannot afford or economically justify a direct selling organization and its home office marketing staff may comprise only a sales or marketing manager who performs many duties. His field selling is usually handled by manufacturers representatives who sell compatible products of other companies, products which have similar market and customer interests. There are many capable, successful manufacturers representatives. They play a very essential part in the sale and distribution of industrial products. Because their fixed overhead and operating costs are shared by at least several other principals, their field selling cost is less than that of a small manufacturer attempting to sell direct. The management of manufacturers representative firms have the same problems of selecting, training and supervising salesmen and most of this book can be utilized effectively by them.

The selection procedure will vary depending on the size and staff capabilities of the company. The subsequent text recognizes this and the procedures will include the point of view of both the small and large industrial selling organizations. Before getting into the details of selection procedures, it is prudent to point out or remind the people who participate in the selection process that there are two points of view involved. The employer concentrates on attracting, evaluating, and selecting new men. The applicant similarly has several objectives. First, he has a natural curiosity about the company which is considering him and which he is considering for what might be a career. There are many questions in his mind and these should be anticipated by the interviewers. In addition to such basic things as the job description, he needs to know about the company and its products, its past history, future growth outlook and competitive position. He is interested in the remuneration opportunities present and future, pension plan and other fringe benefits and, most important, the opportunities for advancement in the company. The enlightened employer recognizes this by giving the applicant pertinent literature about the company and its products and by anticipating these questions by volunteering the information. In other words, he must recognize that this is a two-way selling job, and that if the applicant has outstanding qualifications he undoubtedly is considering other opportunities also.

The sales manager knows the specific qualifications which are essential for success as a salesman in his particular business. Writing the job description is a relatively simple task. The most difficult problem is to select and hire new men who possess a fair complement of these basic qualifications and who appear to have the potential for ultimate success and advancement in sales engineering and marketing. This problem applies equally to the selection of new sales trainees as well as to the selection of applicants who have had previous selling experience. The selection of new trainees usually entails more risk because there is no prior demonstrated selling experience to investigate and factor into the hiring decision. If the applicant is well-qualified in the personality and knowledge categories, the lack of selling experience may be advantageous since it gives the employer the advantage of indoctrinating and training the salesman from scratch.

Under the knowledge category, the applicant's technical educational background and his demonstrated achievements in practice can be probed and their appropriateness for the particular selling job determined. The successful salesman need not have had an outstanding scholastic record, but he should have had sufficient technical knowledge to be able to understand his company's products and their applications in industry.

The selection of salesmen is usually a joint task involving both the field and the home office. It is not unusual for salesmen in outlying territories to be called upon to do the preliminary screening of sales applicants. More frequently, their superior is required to conduct patterned interviews, to administer some basic tests and to make an initial judgment as to whether the applicant is sufficiently qualified to justify the expense of a trip to the home office for further investigation and a final hiring decision.

A typical selection program should include:

1. A simple application form.
2. A preliminary, screening interview.
3. A more comprehensive biographical type of application form.
4. A comprehensive patterned interview.
5. A testing routine.
6. Reference investigations.
7. Summarization and comparison of all impressions, test data, and other inputs.

All of these are important contributions to the final step, the hiring decision.

1. A simple application form

Usually the applicant submits a resumé of some kind outlining his background and experience. This submission may result from an advertisement, an employment agency referral or it may come unsolicited. These resumés rarely give all the information required to decide if a personal interview is warranted. If this is the case, a simple and not too detailed application form should be sent to the applicant with a letter of acknowledgment and a company brochure such as an annual statement. The letter should ask that the application be filled out and returned in advance of an interview appointment. If, based on the resumé information, an immediate interview appears desirable the completed preliminary application should be obtained and reviewed in advance of the personal interview. This initial application should be designed for this purpose and it should include the applicant's vital personal statistics, educational history, recent employment history, military experience or draft status and a statement of the applicant's objectives.

2. The preliminary screening interview

This interview should be basic. The interviewer should tell the applicant something about the company history and the product and market interests. The selling and marketing organization should be explained briefly and a description should be given of the nature and duties of the job. He should state the qualifications for this job. Mention should be made of the advancement opportunities. The applicant should be asked to expand on the information contained in his resumé and the preliminary application. The applicant should be encouraged to talk freely about his work history, why he is seeking a new job or alternatively what prompted him to enter the selling and marketing profession and why he thinks he is qualified for success in this work. The subject of initial and future remuneration opportunities should also be covered briefly. An attempt should be made to determine the applicant's attitude toward the relative importance of security versus advancement which may entail some risks and personal inconvenience. If the interviewer's initial impressions are favorable and the applicant displays active interest he should be asked to take the next step, which comprises filling out a comprehensive, biographical application form.

3. Comprehensive biographical application form

This application usually comprises four pages and it asks for detailed information regarding the applicant's personal and family background, information relative to his education record, experience and work record, previous remuneration, military service record, physical data, civic, social, and professional activities and lastly the applicant's aims and objectives. Standardized forms for this purpose may be obtained from professional book stores that handle psychological tests and supplies. This comprehensive application may be filled out by the applicant at his home and mailed in prior to the next step, the patterned interview.

4. The patterned interview

Looking back now, the first three steps should have provided sufficient basis to decide whether the applicant is worth further processing. If not, he should be discretely and politely eliminated. If, following a review of the biographical application and some verification by specific reference checks if required, he should be invited to visit the home office where the final processing is accomplished. The principle on which patterned interviews are based is that what a person will do in a given job is determined by his basic habits, some of which develop in early life and are virtually unchangeable. A careful, oral review of what the applicant has done in all areas of his life will reveal some basic habit patterns. With this picture of what he has done, it is possible to predict what he may do in the future. The patterned interview may be conducted with more than one interviewer present, thus getting the benefit of two people's opinions regarding the suitability of the applicant. This interview is the only lengthy one and it is followed by a psychological testing routine.

5. A testing routine

As an adjunct to a description of specific tests available it would be well to mention some of the characteristics of successful salesmen that can be measured.

A. Test for mental ability

This shows up in alertness or speed in thinking, quality of thinking and manner of following instructions, all of which are definite factors that are very significant in selling. Such tests of the numerical and verbal type are commonly referred to as intelligence tests. Probably the best known of these are the Otis Self Administering Tests of Mental Ability. The author has utilized the Higher Examination Form C which is appropriate for college graduates. This test normally requires about 30 minutes to complete. It is self administering and it should be taken in the interviewer's office. It can be scored easily and can reveal the applicant's weakness as far as mental ability is concerned.

B. Personality tests

These are used in an effort to ascertain strengths or weaknesses in several character traits.

Emotional stability — the ability to take turndowns without losing self-control or becoming depressed.

Self sufficiency — the ability to work without direction and to be resourceful in meeting new situations and in attacking problems.

Dominance — the ability to control and direct interviews and the persistence to follow through regardless of the obstacles which may impede progress toward getting the order.

Objective-mindedness — the ability to interpret and express facts without being influenced by the personal point of view.

Self-confidence — belief in one's ability to achieve what he undertakes.

These are the most essential personality traits and the absence of one or more of them may be sufficient to disqualify the applicant. Other essential traits include: a sense of humor, tact and diplomacy, and sociability.

It would be unrealistic to expect psychological tests to assess all of these traits accurately. All of them can be double checked in the Patterned Interview and Reference Checking selection phases. Some well known personality tests include the Bernreuter Personality Inventory, the Minnesota Multiphasic Personality Inventory and Social Preference and Behavior Tests. These tests take time to administer. The latter two combined require approximately one hour.

C. Interest tests

These are designed to reveal the applicant's basic interests. The fact that he has applied for a selling position is not in itself evidence that this is really what he wants to do or what he should do. Men sometimes choose selling with a superficial understanding of what it actually entails. They may look at the "glamorous" aspects such as high income and travel and entertainment opportunities. They may not realize the hard work involved and the need for the personality traits described earlier. A typical test in this category is the Strong Vocational Interest Blank. This is used widely and it requires about forty-five minutes to complete. It is particularly valuable in sizing up a recent college graduate or someone who may wish to transfer to selling from an engineering or production career.

D. Achievement tests

These are intended to check the applicant for special knowledge and abilities which he claims and which are essential to the position for which he is being considered. They may involve knowledge of electronics, physics, mechanics and mathematics; and tests are available for these and other categories. Another typical test which is utilized for sales engineering applicants is the Michigan Vocabulary Profile Test. The applicable sections of this test require about 20 minutes time.

E. Selling aptitude tests

Tests in this category are probably the least reliable. Some psychologists offer tests that are a comprehensive, overall measure of the many essential traits which have been described earlier in the text. Many companies administer such aptitude tests of their own design. They are used for special purposes and are usually given in addition to the basic tests.

Psychological tests should not be used as the sole or dominant factor in selecting salesmen. When utilized properly they can play an important part in the selection process. They constitute only one of the essential selection steps described earlier and all of these steps must be factored into the final hiring decision.

6. Reference investigations

When properly conducted, reference checks can constitute a valuable phase in the selection procedure. To be effective they should be carefully designed and phrased to encourage frank and objective responses. Such checks may be made by correspondence, by telephone or—if the job warrants—by personal contact with the pertinent individuals. The correspondence method is effective if specific questions are listed. The recipient may give more valid responses when he considers the questions deliberately and puts his thoughts in writing. Telephone checks are easier and quicker to make. An outline of questions should be used in this connection also. The reference may be more voluble when responding orally but he may also unknowingly place abnormal emphasis on minor points. There may also be a reluctance to make negative comments which may be detrimental to the applicant's interests. The personal visit technique is best, but unfortunately, it is usually impractical where long distances are involved. Realistically conducted reference checks are an indispensable phase of the selection procedure.

7. Summarization

Usually if all of the steps have been performed carefully, it is possible to reach a decision quickly. The applicant's qualifications should be compared critically with the specific job requirements and, if there are several competing applicants, the qualifications should be tabulated and comparisons made. The several interviewers should be invited to express their opinions and make recommendations. If the position to be filled is a key one in the marketing staff, it may be prudent to have the concensus candidate interviewed by an outside psychological testing firm. The examiner would be given, in advance, all available data except the supervisor's conclusions. Consultants who make a specialty of this have experience and complete objectivity in forming a judgment. If the recommended tests are administered, the same consulting firm may be called upon to score the tests.

Supervisory and Performance Review Practices

An essential element in the professional development of the sales engineer and his supervisor is an understanding and appreciation of the purpose and need for field sales supervision. He should be familiar also with the methods used in making performance reviews and appraisals. The salesman and his supervisor have different points of view on this subject but they both have a common interest in the ultimate objective of self-improvement and professional progress. Top management has a fundamental interest because of the substantial amount of money invested in the salaries and expenses of the field organization. Management knows that regular, periodic performance evaluation and appropriate, related controls invariably lead

COUNSELLING
AND
COACHING

to a higher standard of performance from all salesmen. More sales per selling expense dollar can mean an increase in company sales growth rate profit.

There are many reasons for measuring salesmen's performance. One is to appraise and improve the quality and the effectiveness of the job being done. Many salesmen do not perform as well as they can and they benefit from the appraisal and control of their supervisors. Such performance reviews make it possible to determine more realistically the worth and compensation of the men. They also help to point out the men who are worth promoting.

The factors most frequently considered in the performance appraisal include:

1. Sales volume.
2. Ratio of selling expense to sales volume.
3. Ability to carry out planned sales objectives.
4. New account development—creative selling.
5. Knowledge of products and applications.
6. Management of himself and his sales territory.
7. Consistency and accuracy in reporting.
8. Customer relations.
9. Personal qualities.

Assuming the prior establishment of realistic goals, the first four factors listed above are usually considered the most important in making the final judgment of the salesman's ability and worth.

Earlier the salesman was asked to look at himself and to compare his strengths and weaknesses on a trait-by-trait basis. In keeping with the self-development philosophy, the salesman should initiate and periodically make an appraisal of his personal progress. There are many self-rating procedures available but the salesman is best qualified to judge his progress with respect to his own goals.

A typical self appraisal exercise might include such items as:

1. Planning—the ability to do a thorough preparation job in the pre-approach step to a sale. Equally important is regular and careful planning of his daily schedule and also advance planning for the entire week's work. The advance planning should be premised on the territory evaluation and relative account priorities which resulted from the sales territory analysis and planning method. The goal of all of this planning effort is, of course, to utilize his limited face-to-face selling time for maximum sales productivity.

2. Drive—planning on a short or long range basis is meaningless unless the salesman energetically drives to carry out his plans. Drive is to some extent an inborn trait and one which attracts the individual to the selling profession. Without a conscientious effort and a display of enthusiasm and energy in making his rounds, the salesman is not likely to attain marked success.

3. Resourcefulness—the salesman must be able to develop a strategy for handling the variety of situations relative to developing new business, where the idea of using his type of products has to be sold first. Selling against the obstacle of long established competition frequently requires a strategic, novel approach which must be devised on short notice. In other words, the salesman must be imaginative and he must have the ability to think fast as new situations develop.

4. Observation—entails many things and it results from a curiosity leading to the exploration of new business opportunities. This curiosity may also include keeping an eye on his competitors' product quality claims and their activities with respect to the larger customers in the territory. Keeping alert for new and novel applications for his products also comes under this heading.

5. Self development—a salesman must be aware of the need and importance for a continuing self-development program. He must strive to keep up in his knowledge of his company's products and their applications and he should do some outside reading to keep abreast of the technology changes in his particular area of interest. A conscientious effort should be made to develop greater skills in all aspects of selling.

6. Perseverence—means the determination to follow through aggressively in the pursuit of an order in spite of the obstacles and temporary set-backs which may be encountered.

7. Ambition—each man should set a goal for himself and follow it

vigorously. Typically, such a goal would be advancement in his profession — promotion to a field supervisory position and eventually to a higher administrative job in the home office sales and marketing staff.

8. Product demonstrations — present the best tests for the salesman's selling skills. Careful preparation, practice and rehearsal, all contribute to the effective product demonstration.
9. Objective handling — ability to detect and to overcome obstacles or stated objections in a cool, deliberate manner.
10. Order closing — a sense of timing and the use of the most important customer benefit and loss points typify the expert order closer. Here, perseverence is a very necessary ingredient.

The salesman's supervisor, who may be referred to as the branch, district, or regional manager, plays an important role in stimulating his salesmen's progress. Typically, he is charged with:

1. Getting salesmen to utilize consistently the product knowledge and selling tools which they have been taught and trained to use.
2. Guiding and stimulating the salesmen to improvement.
3. Motivating the salesmen in order to help them achieve their sales goals.

A most important tool of the accomplished supervisor is the appraisal and counselling of his salesmen. To do this realistically the following steps are essential.

1. Defining the salesman's job responsibility
   This includes reaching a clearly defined, mutually agreed upon understanding of what is expected of the salesman in terms of his territory, his customers, the products for which he is responsible, and sales goals by customer and product. This definition also includes the salesman's compensation plan and his selling expense budget. Some companies attempt to stipulate a sales territory profit objective also.
2. Measuring the salesman's performance
   This is done in terms of sales volume, territory, and specific account penetration versus competition, and product and market coverage. It may also include the number of sales calls, new accounts sold, the handling of customer complaints and the adherence to his selling expense budget.
3. Counselling and coaching
   Performance measurement or appraisal must be discussed

frankly and factually with the salesman. This is sometimes difficult, and, therefore, it is not always carried out conscientiously.
An important objective of the appraisal interview is to gain the
salesman's acceptance of this measurement. Only then can a
corrective program be worked out in a cooperative manner.
The salesman must want to improve his performance and he
should always play a major role in determining the future course
of action. This plan must be clearly defined and it should
include suggested methods for its accomplishment.

4. Following through

 Performance measurement and appraisal interviews must be
conducted on a programmed, continuing basis to insure maximum benefit to the salesman and the company. Failure to follow
through and continue interest in the salesman's progress may
have a negative effect on his morale and performance.

A typical appraisal form should include the following broad subject
categories:

1. Personality traits — strengths and weaknesses should be noted.
2. Job knowledge — includes knowledge of company and competitive products, application technology, company policies,
   territory, and individual customer intelligence.
3. Territory management — territory analysis and the ability to
   develop and carry out short and long range territory coverage
   and specific customer development programs are the most
   important criteria. Territory and call records, handling of reports
   and correspondence, utilization and maintenance of selling aids
   and demonstration equipment also fall under this heading.
4. Salesmanship ability and performance — these are judged by the
   salesman's knowledge and consistent application of the fundamentals of salesmanship. Of particular importance is the continuing improvement of skills in applying these fundamentals.
   Creativeness and initiative in planning and carrying out novel
   demonstration and sales programs should be important criteria.
   Obviously, the directly measurable factors such as quota
   attainment and selling expense management should be included.

The foregoing outline of typical performance review and counselling procedures is intended to apply to the periodic get-togethers
of the salesman with his supervisor in the local sales office. Many
companies supplement this with a much more comprehensive performance appraisal which includes factors other than sales accomplishment and expense control performance. These are usually made
annually and are reviewed and kept on file in the home office. An

attempt is made to rate the man under the ten categories which comprise the typical annual review:

1. Knowledge of company products, prices, and advertising and sales promotion programs
2. Ability to plan and organize work and to use time wisely
3. Thoroughness and accuracy of reports and records of calls
4. Relationship with the trade, user companies, original equipment manufacturers, distributors and contractors
5. Initiative and creativeness displayed in performing the selling job.
6. Interest and an aggressive attitude toward the job
7. Judgement and common sense
8. Ingenuity in obtaining reports of competitive activities, new models, prices
9. Personal appearance
10. Personal financial affairs

Some companies have developed a system of rating the salesman under these ten categories and using it as a basis of comparison on a year to year basis. This annual appraisal also may influence or help determine changes in the remuneration of the individual. Some companies employ a similar annual review of their field supervisors. These may contain many of the same headings plus a few additional ones which refer to the training and leadership capabilities displayed in their territories. Such appraisals would be initiated by the field sales manager or they may be handled by the regional sales manager. The appraisals are usually reviewed by the regional manager or field sales manager and serious shortcomings, if any, are discussed with the local supervisor.

The objective of this chapter has been to remind both the supervisor and the salesman of the reasons behind the periodic performance reviews, the fundamentals of what they should contain and to dispell any apprehensions or embarrassment on the part of either party to participate in them with a completely frank and cooperative attitude.

Part 4
The Home-Office Marketing Function

What is Marketing?

Industrial marketing may be defined succinctly as ascertaining, creating, and satisfying the needs of the users and manufacturers of industrial products, and doing it at a profit. There are six important requirements for successful marketing:

1. Anticipating the needs and desires of industry and satisfying them as quickly as possible.
2. Early recognition of changes in processing technology in all pertinent industrial markets.
3. Being ready to satisfy these new requirements with appropriate new products, product modifications or services.
4. Recognizing as soon as possible the impact of impending major changes in the business tempo of certain markets which can result in sharply reduced requirements for the company's products. (Government supported markets are a typical example of this).
5. Continuing, full-time effort to diversify and expand the company's product and market interests to insure continuing profitable sales growth.
6. Periodic reviews of the concept of the marketing and selling organization and its effectiveness and appropriateness for current conditions.

In the preceding section we have been concerned with what might be termed the dynamic phase of the marketing function, i.e., the physical aspects of selling the products to industry.

This section will be concerned principally with the marketing functions performed at the home office. These functions are important to the accomplishment of the sale, because they provide essential support to the field sales organization.

The Sales and Marketing Manager

The title of the chief executive in charge of selling and marketing has little uniformity in industrial companies. The size of the company sometimes influences this man's title. In small companies he may be called the Sales Manager, Marketing Manager, or Director of Marketing. Some large companies use the title, Vice President for Sales or Vice President for Marketing. The most realistic and definitive title is Vice President for Sales and Marketing. In the largest multi-division companies there is a chief selling and marketing executive for each manufacturing division and also a corporate marketing director who has largely staff responsibilities.

For our purposes we will call him Chief Executive in Charge of Selling and Marketing, and we will assume that he is employed by a medium sized, single division company whose sales volume justifies a typical selling and marketing organization embracing all of the usual functions. This chief executive is literally responsible for everything which can be related to the selling and marketing categories. In the small company, he may have to handle all of these duties himself. In the typical medium-size company he delegates most of these duties to a diversified supporting staff. These delegated duties and responsibilities will be described in detail as a representative organizational structure is developed.

Therefore, the following list of duties of our simulated Chief Marketing Executive will include only those broad areas for which he is held chiefly responsible by his superior, the chief executive officer. These are summarized briefly as follows:

1. To manage and exercise control of all the selling and marketing activities of the company.
2. To develop, build and maintain a capable, talented selling and marketing organization and to motivate this staff by personal leadership, adequate compensation and appropriate incentives.

3. To supervise and control overall selling expense from the preparation of the budget through to its proper disbursement.

4. To appraise and stimulate efforts to expand current markets for existing products and to seek and exploit new markets. This may be accomplished by recommending the development of new products within the realm of the company's capabilities or by licensing or acquisition.

5. To maintain sales volume at selling prices which will ensure profitable operations.

6. To participate in trade association and industry conferences, and in technical society and professional marketing associations in order to keep abreast of pertinent developments.

7. To serve on, and actively participate in, committee activities as requested by the chief executive officer of the company.

8. To supervise the preparation of reports comparing actual sales accomplishments by products and markets versus the corresponding earlier forecasts. To aid top management in the establishment of sales goals.

9. To participate in the evaluation and approval of all research and development projects which relate to new products or product improvements and which will have an impact on sales progress.

10. Recognizing and alerting management as early as possible to the impact on sales of impending major changes in the tempo of certain markets — changes which can result in sharply reduced demands for certain products.

11. To cooperate with other concerned company executives both by personal contact and through his marketing staff personnel.

12. To make every effort to diversify and expand the company's product and market interests to ensure a sustained profitable growth.

These responsibilities are by no means all-inclusive. Much of this work load is performed by members of the staff along with their other specific duties.

Typical Organization Structures

This figure represents a typical company organization chart. Its purpose is to show all the functional divisions and the relationship of marketing to the other major functions. The President or Chief Execu-

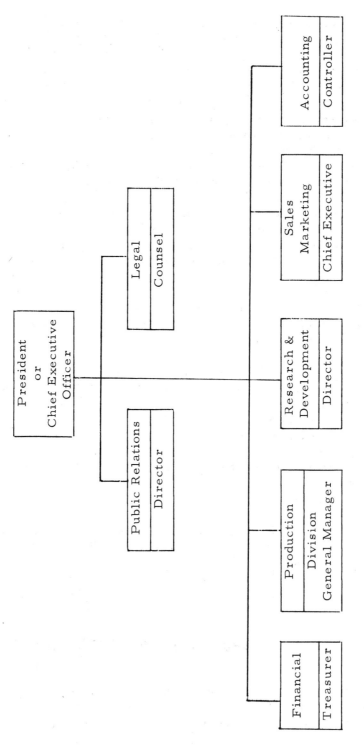

COMPANY FUNCTIONAL ORGANIZATION DIAGRAM

tive Officer is the top man. In large multi-division corporations this man may carry the title of Division Vice President and General Manager. The Public Relations man and Legal Counsel serve the President and work with the five line operating functional chiefs. For example, the marketing chief would work closely with the public relations director on certain kinds of publicity which may have an impact on sales. The legal counsel would advise him on contractual matters, distributor franchises and sales representative agreements, facility rentals. The diagram illustrates the inter-dependency of all operating functions, since each has equal status with the others.

This figure portrays a typical sales and marketing organization for a single division corporation or for a small multi-division corporation which utilizes a single sales and marketing force to handle the products of all divisions. Many medium size corporations are organized in this manner.

This is a typical organization chart for a large multi-division corporation. As corporations expand and add divisions as the result of growth by diversification or acquisition, it becomes necessary to change their organization structure materially. Each division becomes more self sufficient and can justify having its own complete management staff including a Sales and Marketing Director. A corporate staff is formed, including the functions illustrated at the top of the diagram. All of these corporate officers operate in a purely staff capacity and they assist the chief executive officer by observing the performance of their functions in the divisions and by keeping him informed of their progress. Many of their activities involve communication and coordination to avoid conflicts or costly duplication of effort. The research and development, marketing and new business development are typical areas where such coordination is desirable.

The corporate marketing director is concerned with publicity, corporate-wide advertising and promotion. He works closely with the marketing research and new business development managers whose services are available to all divisions. He maintains liaison with the division's sales and marketing directors. He may comment and offer suggestions to them, but he does not have line authority or responsibility for their operations. Some corporations utilize area vice presidents who report to the corporate marketing director. These vice presidents are located in selected regional sales offices and their principal duties are of promotional and prestige nature. They call on the executives of large customers who may buy from several divisions. They may assist by coordinating the efforts of several division supervisors in soliciting large orders and contracts. In the eyes of the customer, they represent top corporate management.

This change from a horizontal organization to a vertical structure usually has the greatest impact on the sales organization. Previously

123

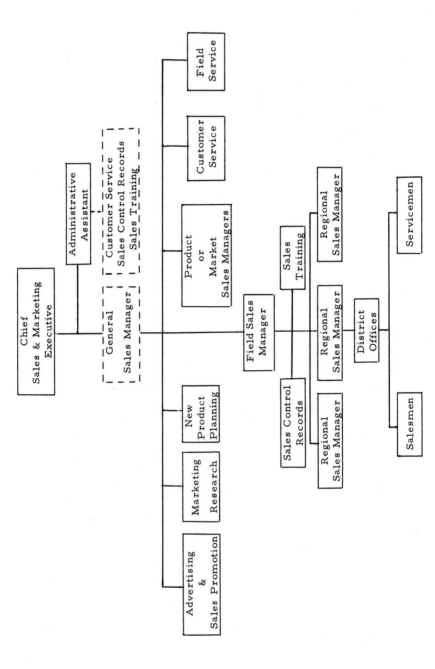

THE MARKETING ORGANIZATION

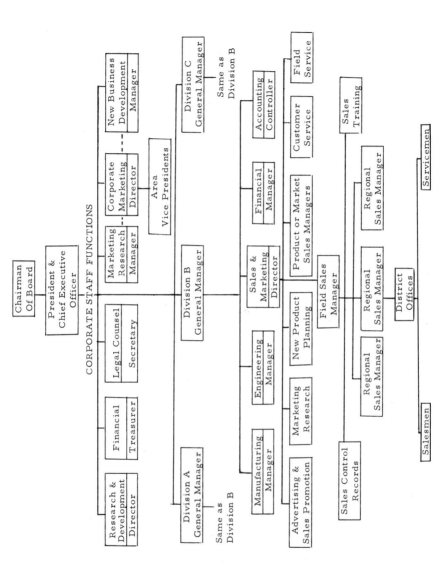

CORPORATE AND MULTI-DIVISION ORGANIZATION STRUCTURE

they have been responsible for the sales and marketing of the products of all the divisions and the top sales executive reported directly to the chief executive officer. Following the change, the sales executive reports to the division general manager who is responsible, exclusively, for his division's products. This change usually necessitates the re-assignment of some salesmen and field supervisors to other divisions where the adjustment by the individuals involved may be frustrating and difficult. Many companies have survived this transition and the economic advantages of the vertical organization form have been realized.

The following explanation of the sales and marketing functions applies to both the horizontal and vertical structures. The only difference in the vertical structure is the change in reporting responsibility of the chief sales executive from the corporate chief executive officer to the division general manager.

Line Versus Staff Responsibilities

It is important to understand clearly the differentiation between line and staff responsibilities. In the home office, only the chief sales executive, the general sales manager and the field sales manager have line responsibilities.

The Administrative Assistant serves primarily in a staff capacity and may perform a wide variety of tasks for the marketing chief. He is concerned with many purely administrative tasks and he serves in a liaison capacity in communicating and helping to carry out directives from the chief to the other functional heads. Shown below him in a dotted line staff relationship are the Customer Service, Sales Control Records, and Sales Training functions. In some company organizations, he is given line responsibility for these groups. This is usually done when the sales volume and manpower size cannot justify the General Sales Manager position, which is shown in a dotted line box for this reason. The sales control records and training responsibilities are usually assigned to the Field Sales Manager.

The General Sales Manager position is a very essential one in large industrial companies whose sales are in the hundreds of millions dollar category. Such companies usually have both Product and Market Managers who require direction and close supervision. This, plus the control of the six other staff operating groups shown imposes a communication and personal supervisory work load which the marketing chief would not have time to perform along with his direct duties and the time consuming conferences involving his superior and the other corporate function managers shown in the horizontal structure. The General Sales Manager serves in a line capacity and it is his responsibility to direct and supervise the marketing organization and see to it that the defined responsibilities and goals are carried out. He must be an outstanding leader who can keep his staff inspired and highly motivated. The usual prerequisite for this job is extensive field sales experience. He must have proven leadership capability and, of course, a thorough knowledge of the pertinent industrial markets and product applications. Almost without exception he is promoted from the field. Another logical progression is from the Field Sales Managership position. In either event, the experience gained in the General Sales Manager position serves to broaden his knowledge in all phases of marketing and it may lead the way ultimately to the top marketing assignment. His responsibilities as General Sales Manager parallel those of the marketing chief to a large extent. The principal difference is that he is a line boss and he is concerned primarily about carrying out programs, objectives and policies. His superior is more concerned about setting objectives and making policy.

With the exception of the Field Sales Manager, all of the other marketing functions are of strictly staff nature.

Product and Market Sales Managers

Some companies use product sales managers while others orient their home-office sales support by markets or industries. There is no one right way to approach this problem. Some companies use product sales managers because they offer a number of product lines which have very little similarity in the market. A company manufacturing heavy duty industrial compressors, gas turbines, and specialty valves will be most likely to use product sales managers. The compressors are high-priced items and skill must be exercised in specifying and applying them. Their market can usually be readily defined so the product sales manager acquires specialized market and customer experience also. To ask him to handle gas turbines or specialty valves, products which are not compatible with a compressor installation and which probably may be used in different industry markets, would reduce his effectiveness. In some companies, product managers have application engineering responsibilities also.

Market or industry sales managers, as they are sometimes called, are concerned with the total requirements for the company products in a specific industry or market segment. Frequently, these products are compatible and they may be sold as a system. Typical examples of market manager categories include petro-chemical, food, textile, paper, metal-producing, and metal-processing. Some other categories are distributor sales and original equipment manufacturer sales. These men know their particular markets thoroughly and they also become acquainted, personally, with the larger customers in that market. They spend considerable time in the field calling on the large accounts with the salesmen and they hold product and market education and training meetings in the field.

In the home office, the product or market sales managers perform many more important duties. They cooperate with and assist the advertising group by suggesting product and product application advertisements. They may cooperate in the design of catalogues, specification sheets and other sales literature. They sometimes write articles regarding product theory or novel product applications for publication in the trade papers or in the company house organ. They may collaborate with the marketing research group in directing or conducting a special survey in which they have pertinent experience. They attend product committee meetings and advise on product improvements and new product considerations. They participate in the preparation of product and market sales forecasts and the geographical or account-by-account distribution of the resulting sales quotas. They may also assist the customer service group in the preparation and pricing of large sales quotations or bids. Thus, it is obvious that these men play a vital role in the marketing function. Their qualifications and motivations are predominantly in the technical areas although they should possess personality traits which are essential to handling customer contacts easily and tactfully. They function in a staff capacity and they must work either through the General Sales Manager or the Field Sales Manager to make specific requests to the field organization. They also work through the Field Sales Manager in developing and coordinating field trip itineraries in order to avoid conflict or duplications of visits by other product or market managers on such trips. In the field, they work closely with the local district managers and salesmen.

Customer Service

This important function is identified by a variety of titles such as Quotation and Order Department, or Sales Engineering Group, but the duties and responsibilities involved are quite similar. This group is the principal communication link between the customers and the home office. Predominant among its duties is the handling of sales inquiries and customer orders. Inquiries are received and analyzed here. These come from the field offices and also direct from the customers and prospects. They may entail simple product literature requests or they may request price and delivery quotations based on specifications which are a part of the inquiry. If these customer inquiries cover standard products and require no application engineering, they are quoted promptly and copies are directed to the field office and to the sales control records group. The more complex inquiries may be referred to the field salesmen for some investigation of the application and qualification of the product specifications. Large projects involving both contracting engineering firms and large industrial plant users may be reviewed also by the product or market manager or by the engineering department prior to quoting.

Records are kept of all communications and it is common practice to employ a follow-up system to ascertain the status and the ultimate disposition of the quotation. If an order results, it is screened and checked for completeness and then written up in a format for use by the production and shipping departments. Customer delivery information requests are usually handled in this group by several people who have close communication with the production scheduling and shipping departments. Preparing quotations and entering orders comprise the major functions but the customer service group is the focal point for most correspondence and it handles a wide variety of other requests from the customers and the field organization. Many home office sales training programs include assignment of the trainee to this group for a limited period of time before he is assigned to a field office. This can serve a dual purpose. The experience gained by such participation will be useful in his eventual field selling assignment. A second and equally important purpose is to provide a reserve pool of men who can be assigned to the field on short notice to fill vacancies as they occur in the field. Many customer service groups are organized on a geographical area basis and sales trainees are assigned to the area sections from which they were hired. This gives them an opportunity to become familiarized in advance with the customers and with the area field supervisors.

Field Service

There are two aspects of field service: the home office staff function, and the field service line function. The home office staff group reports to the chief sales executive or to his subordinate, the General Sales Manager. The field service men report to their local branch supervisors and come under the general administration of the Field Sales Manager as indicated in the horizontal and vertical charts.

The field service function provides an essential and desirable adjunct and support to the selling function. It is an indispensable home office function in large companies as well as small companies whose sales volume cannot afford a field service organization. This group is the focal point for all communications relating to product difficulties ranging from malfunctions within the warranty period to emergency break-downs in the field. It provides necessary liaison between the industrial user and the engineering, production and quality assurance departments in the factory. In this connection, it reviews all reports of individual service calls made in the field and it records and reports to the factory recurring product failures. It may make suggestions for product improvements. When policy questions arise regarding the extent of the company's responsibility, it discusses them with the home office staff and field people involved and recommends the resulting conclusions to the factory department.

Many large companies offer periodic field maintenance service for users who do not have qualified repair men. Such arrangements usually entail service agreements which stipulate the frequency and the time spent on such calls. The charge for this service is agreed upon in advance and usually includes all expenses involved except the cost of replacement parts. This periodic service provides preventive maintenance for the user at a moderate cost. Its benefit of insuring customer satisfaction has obvious sales advantages. The home office service group monitors and keeps records of these periodic service activities.

Another typical function is the training of men for the field service assignment. This is usually done in collaboration with the sales training supervisor, and a common facility is used. Many progressive companies offer similar training opportunity for maintenance employees of their large customers. Such training is usually offered on a no charge or a cost basis. Training of this nature enhances customer relationships and provides a significant customer benefit as well as a sales advantage.

The Field Sales Manager and his Organization

The Field Sales Manager is a very important member of the home office marketing organization. In large companies, he reports directly to the General Sales Manager. In smaller operations he may report directly to the Sales or Marketing Manager. The importance of his job is rated in this same sequence. His prime qualification is extensive field sales experience, and he usually progresses from field sales engineer to district or branch manager, and then to regional sales manager. Promotion to the Field Sales Manager position usually results from demonstrated competence as a field supervisor plus evidence of other qualifications which will enable him to grow and advance further in marketing management. Outstanding performance in this initial home office assignment plus the experience gained in the other marketing functions can qualify this man for advancement to the General Sales Manager or Sales Manager position.

As shown in the horizontal chart, the Field Sales Manager has principally line responsibility. He has complete control of the field sales and service activities, working through the regional and district sales offices. He also supervises the maintenance and distribution of key customer records and the monitoring of sales control procedures and salary records. He is responsible for the sales training function. These latter groups will be discussed in greater detail later in the text. First, we will review some of the other important duties which he is required to perform.

The most important one is to build, maintain and manage an efficient, well qualified and highly productive field sales and service organization. In this connection, he determines and recommends to his superior the size and structure of the field organization, the extent of specialized sales effort by product, market or customer category and the use of other supplementary distribution channels. If manufacturers representatives are used, for complete or supplementary sales coverage, it is his responsibility to select them and to administer them much as he would a directly employed sales force.

He has the prime responsibility for recommending the form or method of remuneration for his people, for collaborating in devising the plan and for administering such a plan. This is an extremely important duty because of its impact on the sales productivity and morale of the field men. He also determines the compensation basis for manufacturers representatives and negotiates agreements with them.

It is his responsibility to help plan specific sales programs and to see that they are carried out in the field. In this connection, he determines and assigns sales quota objectives by regions and branches and he assists the branch manager in determining the salesmen's individual quotas. The distribution of the regional quotas is done with the assistance and cooperation of the regional and branch managers. These quotas represent the geographical distribution of the overall national sales forecast goal which has been developed cooperatively in the home office and finalized by the marketing chief and his superior.

As a parallel function, he recommends and assists in the preparation of selling expense budgets. His office determines the geographical distribution of budgets and monitors their enforcement. It reviews and approves travel and other selling expense reports for the people who report to him.

Another very important duty is to supervise the recruitment, hiring and training of sales personnel under his jurisdiction. He works closely with the regional and branch managers in the final interview and employment agreement phase. When they are available, he utilizes the applicable talents of his company's employment department.

It is his responsibility to help in the planning and administering of periodic sales meetings at the regional and home offices. The purpose of such meetings is to provide training in new products and applications, to present salesmanship refresher courses and to motivate and stimulate the sales force.

In the home office, he makes suggestions for new and improved products and for obsoleting old products. He informs management of important competitive developments which are observed in the field, and he reports significant changes in the activity of the various industrial markets. He assists in planning the system for reporting sales by products and markets and in comparing these with the established quota goals.

It is his responsibility to coordinate the itineraries of field visits planned by the market sales managers. This is done to avoid conflicts and duplication of visits and to avoid excessive demands on the field which might seriously reduce the salesman's customer contact time.

He participates in various home-office committee activities as directed by his superior and he cooperates with other department heads on matters having mutual interest and concern. One example of this could be in the joint utilization of a training facility and the audio-visual training aids which are the property of another department.

Sales Control Records

The maintenance and distribution of certain records and reports which are essential for sales control purposes is normally the responsibility of the field sales manager. Sales control records entail only those categories which are essential for the evaluation and control of the field organization. They are the necessary tools for use by the branch and regional managers and by the field sales manager. They contain vital, up-to-date information which helps these individuals to perform their supervisory duties. They should not be confused with the purely statistical reports covering such things as product sales by models, sales by industrial market categories, overall industry sales, general business indicators and service records.

Typically, these records include:

1. Sales performance—sales by region, branch and salesman, usually issued on a monthly basis. They are compiled and distributed as soon as possible. They usually cover both incoming orders and shipments since the latter may be the basis for the incentive increment of the field men's income.

2. Forecast and quota accomplishment—are usually issued quarterly. They compare quarterly shipments with branch and regional quota goals, and the total shipments are compared with the overall national forecast.

3. Selling expense versus budget—monthly reports that break down the field expenses by branch and regional territories. Comparisons are made with the budgeted expenses on a monthly and year-to-date basis. The branch manager may further detail these, based on local records, and review that portion of the expenses which relate to the individual salesman.

4. Sales call reports—monthly or quarterly summarization of the number of calls made by the salesmen by branch. This is done in the branches and only the summaries are sent to the home office. These reports have value to the home office but they also serve to remind the salesman that his prime purpose is to spend most of his time with his customers and prospects. It is a quantitative rather than a qualitative measurement.

5. Business activity contact reports—individual sales call reports which involve only large negotiations. They constitute job sta-

tus or progress reports on important, large quotations and they are sent in daily. The format used permits rapid data processing by the home office and the resulting summary reports are disseminated quickly to the field supervisors and to all home-office personnel who need this intelligence and who may be able to help by making concessions in delivery or pricing. A master file of these reports is kept at the home office.

6. Lost business reports—submitted by the salesman and reviewed at the home office.

7. Key customer records—key customer profiles that are maintained in the branch and home offices. They are updated periodically by individual sales contact reports. Business volume obtained is posted periodically at the home office and a copy of the updated report is sent to the field offices. These important records of sales progress with the key customers—who usually contribute at least two-thirds of the new equipment sales—are reviewed by the product and market managers and by the field supervisors.

The Sales Training Function

The necessity and value of sales training is recognized by most manufacturers of industrial products. The expense of an appropriate training program is minor when it is compared with the benefits it invariably produces—increased sales and increased profits. The well-trained salesman, with his wide knowledge of products and applications, combined with related skillful selling and marketing in his territory, develops new business and has higher rates of sales than his less-qualified competitors. He develops enduring, favorable customer relationships. Because of his company's continuing efforts to help him develop professionally, he is more likely to stay and to seek advancement within his company.

Despite the general recognition of these broadly stated benefits, too many companies do an ineffective job of sales training. The limited training provided by many companies is done in a perfunctory manner because of urgent field personnel replacement requirements.

The first step in designing a training program is to decide who can benefit and, with resulting increased capability, can produce more profitable sales for the company. The job categories which should be considered include:

1. New and experienced salesmen
2. Selected home office sales and marketing personnel
3. Field service engineers
4. Customer maintenance men

Following this, consideration should be given to the kinds of training which should be offered to provide appropriate instruction for the diverse needs of these job categories. Next the subject matter to be included should be decided and the time requirement for covering these subjects should be estimated. Consideration must be given to the training staff required, the training facility and equipment needs. The expense of the overall training activity should be estimated.

The following types of training are required and they should all be considered when formulating a long range training program and determining the staff and facilities required:

1. An initial, basic training course designed for graduate engineers having the prescribed qualifications for field sales engineering work. These recruits may or may not have had related product or sales experience. This course would be given to all men who are hired for immediate or eventual field sales assignment, regardless of the extent of their previous work experience.
2. An initial, basic training course designed for men who have the qualifications for field service assignment. This course may include some of the product and application sections used in the basic training course outlined above if this is considered practical from the division's standpoint.
3. A continuing, formalized, group training course to be carried out in the field offices. The training department would provide texts, materials, and outlines for such courses which would be administered by the local field office managers. Home-office personnel, including product and market sales managers, application engineers and others would participate in such periodic local training sessions when convenient.
4. On-the-job training, following the initial basic training, for new men who have had no related selling experience. This training might include a period of apprenticeship as an inside sales engineer in a district or regional office or a preliminary assignment as a junior sales engineer assisting and working with an experienced senior salesman prior to being given the responsibility of a sales territory.
5. Home-office refresher training on a regularly scheduled basis. The major purpose of this training would be to bring the field

men to the home office at some regular interval in order to keep them abreast of new developments, company policies, organizational and procedural changes. This training may be informal and should include a minimum of product study. The duration of such programs should not ordinarily exceed one week.

6. A sales management development training program should be offered selectively to those men who have potential for promotion to such positions as District Manager, Regional Manager, Product Sales Manager or Director of Marketing. This training may be done partially on a subsidized basis using outside organizations, talents and facilities, but it should also include participation by home office management people to cover those aspects which are related to the company's products.

7. A home-office marketing personnel training program should be offered to those employees who display aptitudes and interests for outside sales assignments or for promotion to internal marketing positions. This should be done selectively using portions of the initial basic training program (paragraph 1 above) which is designed for sales engineering trainees.

8. A customer training program should be designed and scheduled regularly in accordance with the requirements of the division. The extent of this activity would depend on its value to the division.

In summary, the overall training requirements should provide for field sales engineers, field service engineers, home-office selling and marketing personnel and customer personnel. In order to determine accurately the size of the training facility, some attempt should be made to estimate the number of people in each of these categories who may require training for each of the next five years.

THE INITIAL BASIC TRAINING COURSE

This course is the foundation for all sales and service personnel because it is the most comprehensive course offered. It should be developed with the intent to use texts and audio-visual techniques. The instructors who will do the lecturing and instructing should use standarized texts, and materials which have been prepared by the application engineers, product managers, customer service personnel and other departmental personnel. Direct participation by these marketing and departmental people should be limited to specialized subjects in line with their particular capabilities. Routine coverage of principles, standard and product application information and the like should be handled by a full-time training staff. This will lessen the demands made on the marketing staff and permit them to concentrate on their regular duties in the marketing departments.

A typical curriculum totaling 45-50 days or 9 to 10 weeks should include the following:

Orientation and Indoctrination   (3 days)
This should include familiarization with the corporate and division history, the products, the markets, and the competition. Growth and profit objectives, organization description, insurance, profit sharing and other fringe benefits, and facility inspection tours should also be included. The importance of the salesman in relation to the corporation objectives should be stressed.

Product and Application Study   (20 days)
This should include a brief preliminary description of the products to be studied and their applications with particular stress on their place in industry, a review of the fundamental operating principles used, further orientation covering the markets in which they are sold, and the position of the division in its industry. Detailed study of the products should follow, with lectures supplemented by laboratory sessions which will permit the trainees to operate and adjust the equipment in order to become familiar with the performance characteristics of the various models. A compilation of all available application information should be given to the trainees for home study. Daily and weekly tests should be given to check and measure the trainees' progress.

Pricing, Quotation and Order Procedures   (12 days)
This should include review of quotation and order procedures with reference to the marketing administrative manual, pricing, government bidding and contract negotiation procedures and regulations including policies regarding proprietary information, applicable government regulations and cost accounting for contract negotiation purposes.

Salesmanship   (10-15 days)
This should include study of the fundamentals of salesmanship, the development of a sales manual including specific product and application sales information, the study and practice of selling techniques, sales territory planning, management and development. Some on-the-job training should be provided locally if practical. Five days are provided in the time estimate for this purpose.

ALLOCATION OF THE TRAINING RESPONSIBILITY

As illustrated in the horizontal and vertical charts, the prime responsibility should be given to the Field Sales Manager. Because

137

of his absences for essential field visits, it may be convenient to assign the day to day administration of the training department to the General Sales Manager or to the Administrative Assistant to the chief marketing executive. The development of the various programs, selection of the training department personnel, and other initial planning should be a joint endeavor of a group including the chief executive officer, the Administrative Assistant, the General Sales Manager and the Field Sales Manager. The prime responsibility for the administration and evaluation of the overall program should rest with the Field Sales Manager.

These training recommendations are appropriate for a multi-division corporation with a horizontally structured selling and marketing organization serving small sized product divisions. They are appropriate for the relatively larger divisions of a vertically-structured organization. In the latter situation, it is assumed that each division is large enough to be able to afford its own selling and marketing staff. If the division sales volume cannot support a training organization and facility, it is possible to locate it at the corporate headquarters, under the jurisdiction of the corporate marketing director with the divisions cooperating in the program planning, facility usage and sharing the expenses involved. It would be the responsibility of the corporate training department to collaborate with division marketing management and the departmental personnel to assist them in the design of training courses and the development of required manuals, texts and materials.

ORGANIZATION

The corporate sales training organization should comprise a manager of sales training and one or two training engineers. In addition, one secretary and one clerk-typist would be required initially.

The Manager of Sales Training should have an appropriate technical background plus a background of successful industrial training experience involving technical products in a related industry. Primarily, he should be sales oriented and should preferably have had previous sales experience and field sales training experience. He should be responsible for the establishment and implementation of training programs to insure the maximum effectiveness of the sales effort. In addition to supervision of the training staff, the Manager of Sales Training:

1. Helps to determine the sales training needs for the division--
2. Develops and administers established training plans, programs and procedures--
3. Sets up and maintains training facilities--
4. Prepares reports on the progress of personnel under his direct or indirect supervision during their training periods--

5. May analyze performance of sales personnel to determine whether additional training should be prescribed--
6. Keeps informed on training methods and techniques of competitors and new developments in the training field--
7. May assist in the recruitment of personnel for the sales organization--
8. Assists in developing new training courses as may be required because of introduction of new products--
9. Continually studies and develops skill in the use of better teaching and training methods.

The training engineer also must be technically qualified and he must have had experience as an instructor in some related field. A thorough knowledge of the technology which is used in the company's products would be desirable. He must be capable of assisting in planning and developing training courses, texts and materials.

FACILITIES

A lecture room or rooms, arranged in classroom style, of adequate size for the anticipated number of trainees should be provided. Audio-visual projection equipment, public address system, tape recorder and other required facilities should be included. Rooms should be air-conditioned, and sound and light-proofed, so they can be used simultaneously without interference with each other.

One laboratory area should be provided. This should be of adequate size and should have benches arranged for small group product-operating experiments and demonstrations.

A store room should be provided for training equipment, literature and demonstration instruments.

A training department office area should be provided adjacent to the training facility. This should include a private office for the training manager with partitioned areas for the training engineers and the secretarial staff. Space should be provided for a training reference library and a small conference room which could be used for interviews and individual instruction purposes.

BUDGET ESTIMATE

The extent of the training staff and the nature and size of the facility will vary widely according to the company and the average number of trainees to be processed and the number and kinds of programs to be given. The expense of the training program will vary accordingly, of course. For an organization like the one described, the total annual expense might approximate $50,000 to $60,000 per year.

In assessing the budget requirements, the benefits of the training operation in terms of increased sales volume and increased profits should be emphasized. All companies can afford some type of training for both the beginning and the experienced salesman. If an in-house facility cannot be justified on a full-time basis, there are professionally designed courses available which can provide the salesmanship and marketing instruction and development.

The Remuneration of Salesmen

Determining an appropriate method of compensating the salesmen can be a simple task or a complex, difficult one, depending on the objectives of the employer. The simplest method entails the payment of a straight salary with periodic merit increases based on the sales-

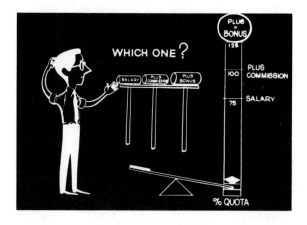

man's overall performance judged by his superiors. The more complex plans provide a base salary, which relates to his job classification, plus commissions and/or bonus payments which relate to his selling accomplishments. The objective of the latter plan is to provide an incentive which will motivate the salesman. Both methods have advantages and disadvantages. The nature and size of the company's business is the major factor in determining which approach is more appropriate.

Some of the more important considerations which relate to the company's business are:

The size of the company in terms of sales volume, the number of salesmen employed, and the diversity of its operations may impose practical limitations because of the possible complexity in designing and administering one of the more effective incentive plans.

The nature of the products handled must be taken into account also. Are they simple or complex? Do they require considerable application engineering assistance? Do they have a moderate value of, say, under $5,000 or a higher unit value amounting to $100,000 or more? If they are simple, standard products, requiring little application assistance, an incentive plan may be practical. If they are complex, have a very high value and require application engineering assistance, the length of time to make such a sale is much greater and a salary plus annual merit bonus plan is usually more practical. In this latter situation, long deliveries may be involved and this would reduce the possibility for short-range motivation effectiveness.

The markets in which the products are sold are also a factor. If they are predominantly industrial, incentive plans are more appropriate. They may be inappropriate where the government markets predominate and where the contract prices may vary widely and the salesman's contribution to the sale is difficult to assess. Another point in this comparison is the limited opportunity for creative selling when large government contracts are involved.

The sales channels used will have some influence on the form of compensation. If most sales are handled on a direct-to-the-user or contractor basis, there is no problem. If the reverse is true and most of the sales are made by distributors, dealers or original equipment manufacturers, a different type of plan should be used.

Another possible complication may be experienced when several salesmen, in different locations, contribute to obtaining the ultimate order. Here sales credit splits are involved and inevitable disputes occur regarding the fairness of the sales credit allocation and the accompanying incentive pay distribution.

After reviewing these considerations and possible problem areas one may question why incentive plans should be considered at all. Wouldn't a salary plus merit increases and a discretionary year end bonus be much simpler? The obvious answer is "Yes" but the decision must give priority to consideration of the company's objectives. If maximum sales per selling expense dollar are desired, many companies have decided that the benefits of directly-related selling incentives far outweigh the work of designing and administering an appropriate plan. The typical salesman needs and enjoys a challenge. Each selling situation provides an opportunity to apply his skills and ingenuity to get the order. His attitude toward his income is similar and he wants it to relate to his accomplishments. Experience has proven that with a true incentive challenge he works much harder, gets more satisfaction from his work, and is a much happier employee.

This has been proven by the marked increase in the number of companies that have switched to salary plus incentive plans in recent years. During the past 15 years the percentage of industrial companies having incentive plans has increased by nearly 50 percent--from usage by 50 percent of the large industrial companies to approximately 75 percent. This shift has been mostly away from straight salary plans but it represents also a departure from straight commission plans which were prevalent years ago.

The sales compensation methods in general use today include salary only, straight commission only and salary-plus-incentive plans. There are many variations of the latter category. Some of these will be described later. Prior to giving consideration to a specific plan, some preliminary steps should be taken.

An approximation should be made of the amount of money available in the selling and marketing budget for the compensation of the salesmen. This amount assumes the attainment of a realistic sales goal. This figure is used for the planning phase since it represents the maximum number of dollars available regardless of the method of compensation. A more realistic yardstick is the percentage of total company sales allowable for field selling expense. For industrial capital goods products this approximates between 5 and 8 percent. A typical percentage for only the field salesman and his travel expense approximates only three percent. The use of comparable percentage figures which reflect the company's actual experience provides a more flexible approach to budgeting and staffing to keep pace with the changing tempo of total sales.

The sales compensation plan may also be geared to the attainment of other company objectives in addition to fulfilling the sales quotas and selling expense budgets. These objectives may include:

1. Creative selling to add new accounts and to broaden the usage of the company's products in existing accounts--
2. Promotion of new products--
3. Thorough exploitation of the sales territories by means of territory analyses, company and competitor account evaluation and better utilization of the available selling time--
4. Cooperation with other salesmen on projects where the buying influence is spread geographically--
5. Self-improvement efforts carried out and displayed by the salesman.

To accomplish all of these objectives may seem idealistic or unrealistic, but they may constitute serious needs for some companies.

The first step in developing a salary plus incentive plan is to define the various grades of salesmen and to establish appropriate base salaries for each category. Such definition usually includes a list of duties and responsibilities for each grade. These descriptions usually cover the sales trainee, the junior or beginner salesman and the senior, experienced salesman. The base salary determination must take into account the percentage of the incentive pay increment which is appropriate and also it should include a comparison of the resulting estimated total compensation with that offered by its principal competitors for comparable jobs.

There are three types of base salary plus incentive plans: fixed salary plus commissions; fixed salary plus bonus; and fixed salary plus commission plus bonus.

In the first category, the fixed salary would approximate the base salary. This should be adequate to cover the salesman's normal living expenses. A small commission would be paid on all sales, with no conditions or exceptions imposed. The commission percentage determination would depend on the amount of sales which the company expects the salesman to contribute in the year ahead. This should be a realistic, attainable total. For example, if the senior salesman produces $300,000 per year normally, the commission percentage on all sales might be set at one percent. Assuming a $10,000 fixed salary, his commission would then amount to $3,000 and his total income would amount to $13,000. His commission would be about 23 percent of his total pay. If credit splits are practiced, the commissions would apply to the salesman's credit share of the total business reported. This would assure equitable rewards to the several salesmen who contributed to getting the order. This type of plan appears to rank second in industry today. Its popularity is exceeded only by the fixed salary plus bonus plan.

Where this plan is used, the fixed salary is higher and the bonus percentage is lower. A typical bonus figure would be ten to fifteen percent of the fixed salary. Bonus payments are usually not directly related to the salesman's order volume. They may be determined on a discretionary, judgment basis in which case they are paid annually. Another method is to pay the bonus as a reward for group performance, thus encouraging cooperation within the branch office. Typically, this might be given for group effort in exceeding the assigned quota for a given quarter. Such payments would be divided equally among the participating salesmen and their supervisors. Some companies limit the distribution of such payments to the salesmen who have attained their individual quotas for the quarter. There are many variations of this plan in use and, currently, it is the most popular — probably because it is the simplest of the several incentive plans to administer.

Fixed salary plus commission plus bonus is used to only a limited extent although in some companies it may have special appeal. Essentially it is a combination of the first two categories. It retains the high incentive attraction of fixed salary plus commission and for this reason it is popular with the salesmen to whom it is applied. The bonus increment would be offered to encourage group cooperation and it is paid for exceeding the branch quarterly sales quota. Some companies size this bonus incrementally with an increasing bonus percentage in steps which relate to how much the quota has been exceeded. In other words, the more the quota is exceeded the higher the percentage bonus paid. When properly designed, this plan can be the most effective one for medium sized companies because of the provision of substantial incentive plus a smaller reward for group cooperation and accomplishment.

In concluding this section it should be re-emphasized that incentive remuneration plans for salesmen are widely used and continue to grow in popularity. The benefits in the form of increased sales productivity and morale in the sales force — usually accompanied by a decrease in field selling expense — can far outweigh the effort expended in designing the plan and in administering it from the home office.

The Marketing Research Function

These two words - marketing research - in themselves provide the best definition of this important staff function. In this form it is applicable to consumer, commercial, and industrial product manufacturers. For convenience the title is usually shortened to market research. This abbreviated title is misleading since it implies the limited function of researching markets only whereas the true definition includes research and investigation of all aspects of marketing the product.

A more detailed definition would comprise generalities since the description of the duties performed varies appreciably for consumer, commercial, and industrial companies. In this chapter we will confine ourselves to the responsibilities, organization and duties performed in an industrial products company.

Referring to the horizontal and vertical organizational charts, it is apparent that market research is wholly a staff function which reports to the marketing chief and which services and cooperates with most of the other marketing staff groups. Depending on the defined job responsibilities and direction given by the marketing chief, the marketing research function may be either a dynamic, imaginative, market expansion-seeking group or a passive source of market information and statistics collected by directive for the benefit of the marketing chief and the other staff groups. Unfortunately, in many companies it falls into this latter passive category.

A typical organization includes a manager and a staff comprising a market analyst, a sales analyst, a statistician and one or more skilled field investigators.

The Group Manager and the Market Analyst individually and jointly perform the most important duties which include:

1. Continuing analyses of the activities and trends in the markets which are the prime buyers of the company's products. This is accomplished by maintaining and studying pertinent trade association statistics and other industry group statistics and business indicators --
2. Analyzing product sales to the various markets and estimating the extent of the company's penetration of these markets --
3. Conducting special market studies to ascertain the technology trends and the requirement for new products or for substantial modification of existing products --
4. Field investigations to check product acceptance on a sampling basis --
5. Keeping current on competitors' activities and new products. This includes maintaining an up-to-date, master file of competitors' product literature, prices and sales volumes --
6. Substantiating or validating the requirements for proposed new products which are being considered --
7. Cooperating in making arrangements for pre-testing new products which are nearing completion --
8. Making specific studies of the effectiveness of advertising campaigns and assisting in the selection of advertising media.

The Field Investigators mentioned earlier handle much of the outside contacts required to carry out these duties.

The duties of the Sales Analyst all relate to the performance of the selling and marketing function. They may include:

1. Evaluating the progress and results of established sales objectives --
2. Studying and monitoring the various selling and marketing costs --
3. Measuring performance against sales quotas. He may also assist in the determination of branch territory and salesmen's quotas --

4. Assists Market Analyst in interpreting and reporting the results of the market and product studies.

The Statistician's chief function is to prepare reports summarizing much of the information gathered by the group and putting it in report forms which can be readily understood by marketing management and by the division and corporate management. These include statistical data for the preparation of forecasts of sales by products and markets. He also analyzes reports of general economic conditions, related business indicators and reports them in usable form to management.

In summary, the marketing research function is an essential supporting service for the marketing and sales management and for several of the other staff marketing groups. It works very closely with the product and market sales managers, the advertising group and the new product planning group. Many of the reports which it produces provide essential intelligence to both the division management and the corporate management.

Business Forecasting and Quota Determination

The intent of this chapter is to explain the forecasting function and to describe in general terms the theories and methods which have been applied by some industrial equipment manufacturers. There is a marked contrast with the methods employed by the engineering and production departments in predicting their respective goals. In these departments, every effort, every consideration eventually comes to focus on this all important problem. In production, the programming of a new product from the research and drafting room stages to the finished product stage is carefully and expertly planned. The engineers and production men have at their disposal measurement and control methods to insure the precision and reliability of the finished product. When the marketing department becomes involved, this element of precision is lost, since the marketing chief must rely on less precise methods and tools to prepare his predictions.

Probably the most difficult and often the most perplexing task of the marketing division is that of accurately forecasting sales. This must be done on an annual short-range basis, and on a long-range basis which usually encompasses a three-to-five-year period. The chief marketing executive usually has the major responsibility for the final forecast. This is then submitted to top management. Here it is subjected to a critical review by the president and his corporate staff, and some adjustments may be made. Following its acceptance it is distributed to the various functional heads who use it as a basis for planning.

These activities include financial budgeting for all operations, production planning, shipment estimates, and dollar requirements for capital equipment and other non-operating expenditures. Last, but most important, an estimate must be made of the year end net income and profits. The short range forecast is somewhat easier to prepare because it is influenced largely by past and current sales history. This is particularly true if adequate records of sales by products, markets and key customers have been maintained in the past. The long-range forecast is much more difficult to prepare because of the uncertainties in the economic outlook. It is used to check and possibly to amend the company's long-range plan. Such plans include plant and personnel expansion, product and market diversification, acquisitions and many other subjects. The short-range, annual forecast is more critical since its accuracy may have a major effect on the company's product performance for the current year.

The marketing chief usually relies on the marketing research group to coordinate and centralize the task of preparing the forecast. Others who share the responsibility and contribute important in-puts are the product and market sales managers, the field sales manager and the regional and branch field supervisors. In a large, decentralized corporation, the division managers are responsible for the forecasts and they are given some latitude with respect to the approach used in arriving at them. The marketing department plays the major role in developing and recommending the forecasts for consideration and finalization by the division and corporate management.

Forecasting is far from being an exact science and there are no infallible procedures which can be applied universally. Companies do a creditable job of pricing, production control, sales and distribution. But in the final analysis they must depend on the forecast to provide the foundation and guidance for these intra-company functions. Unfortunately, some companies do not devote enough time and effort to the development of a sound forecasting procedure. Most companies have factors which are peculiar to their own businesses and they cannot rely fully on forecasting methods which are used generally.

The forecasting approaches employed can be categorized broadly as subjective, objective, and a combination of both. The subjective approach attaches major importance to the company's past history and its current experience. Because it utilizes past and current sales statistics of the company and those of related industry and trade associations, it can predict with reasonable accuracy. Extrapolations and interpretations of such past statistical history provide the foundation for both short and long range predictions. The objective approach looks outside the company experience and takes into account the projections of pertinent business indicators, economic cycle patterns and the company's own objectives in new business development. Most companies use a mixture of the subjective and objective points of view.

The techniques used to produce these forecasts include:

1. Gathering and interpreting intelligence from within the company's records and related sources --
2. Projections of such intelligence by charting, comparison with basic indices and possibly utilizing computer techniques --
3. Final judgment and decision by those who are best qualified and who bear the responsibility to the shareholders for the outcome in terms of annual accomplishment.

Technique number one is, of course, the simplest—assuming that the job of record keeping has been done carefully. Presumably such statistics as sales by products and models, and sales by markets are available covering the past. These may be plotted on a time chart and, by drawing an average line through the points, a projection based purely on past history may be obtained. Industry and trade associations statistics may be used for comparison. In the capital goods industries, the annual purchases of the key customers, past and current, and the outlook for the new year may be assessed on an account by account basis. The total prediction obtained by this method may represent two-thirds or more of the company's total business. This process may be carried out in the branch offices using standardized formats developed by the marketing research group. These key customer records, accumulated over a period of years, can provide a valuable input for each successive annual forecast. They can be used in determining long range forecasts of specific market growth since they are representative of the various markets which the company serves.

The second technique, utilizing intelligence obtained outside the company, can be used for both annual and five-year forecasts. This intelligence may include various leading indicators, among them:

1. New orders in the durable goods industries --
2. Contracts and orders for plant and equipment --
3. New orders in the machinery and equipment industries --
4. Planned and approved capital expenditures for new plant and equipment --

5. Construction contracts awarded for commercial and industrial buildings --
6. Trends in manufacturers' unfilled order backlogs --
7. Government planned expenditure reports --
8. Corporate profits after taxes.

There are also coincident indicators which are issued monthly whose trends may provide a basis for comparison with the current tempo of the company. A few of these are:

1. Industrial production, total and by major industry classes --
2. Gross National Product --
3. Manufacturing and trade sales --
4. Unemployment rate --
5. Backlog of capital expenditures -- manufacturing companies --
6. Manufacturers unfilled orders --
7. Trade association business volume reports.

These leading and coincident indicators are used in a variety of ways. Following some years of observations and comparisons, the marketing research group may identify the several indicators that have paralleled most closely the company's sales history. A typical example of a leading indicator for a manufacturer of industrial equipment is the Planned Capital Expenditures for new plant and equipment. Economic business cycle indicators may be considered also.

The third technique consists of the judgment factor which precedes the final executive decision. The corporate chief executive officer, together with the treasurer, meet with the divisional general manager, his production manager and the chief marketing executive. The marketing research manager may attend to explain and to substantiate some aspects of the forecast. Eventually, concessions may be made and a final decision is reached. The forecast is then reproduced in its final form and is distributed to the department heads for detailed budgeting and production planning.

The chief marketing executive's function does not cease here. The next task is to see that the forecasted sales are distributed geographically as quotas for the regions and the branch territories. The field sales manager plays a major role in assigning these quotas. He is assisted by the marketing research group and by the regional managers. The individual salesmen's quotas are determined jointly by the regional and branch supervisors, subject to approval by the field sales manager. The effect of these new quotas on the salesman's individual and group remuneration plan is determined at this time so that a single announcement can be made covering these subjects.

It should be reiterated that there is no formula which can assure the determination of an accurate forecast. The methods and tools described can provide a framework to guide the marketing division's efforts. By conscientiously applying these suggestions, and using some mature judgment a satisfactory forecast can result. The accuracy of the annual forecast will depend largely on the quality of the records of sales by products, markets and by key customers. This quality will depend on the thoroughness and current validity of the territory analysis procedures and the sales control records — particularly those relating to the key customers — which were described earlier in this section. Furthermore, the prudent marketing chief should check frequently with his marketing research group, to learn the progress of sales accomplishment versus the forecast. If there is significant disagreement, either on the high side or on the low side, it is his responsibility to determine the cause and to alert top management to the possible impact of these variations on the other company departments.

Advertising and Sales Promotion

The major functions of the Advertising and Sales Promotion Department are probably the most readily understood of all of the home-office staff activities. Sales promotion is a specific form of advertising which borders on selling since it relates to certain specific products or services and utilizes various and often novel methods to attract the buyer's attention and to invite his inquiries. Direct mail campaigns, traveling product displays and trade show exhibits fall into this category.

The advertising function provides a most valuable adjunct and support to the selling and marketing activities. It is an important contribution to total selling effectiveness. It is particularly effective in helping to accomplish the attention and interest steps to a sale. This is done by composing advertisements which result in inquiries and thus provide leads for the salesmen. It provides a rapid means of communication to announce new products and to call attention to their good qualities and customer benefits. Prestige advertisements, featuring product usage and outstanding product performance experienced by big name companies, provide the assurance which influences the decision step to a sale.

A listing of the activities and output of this group will further clarify its function and contribution:

1. Advertisements — product, application and prestige-building advertisements for trade magazines and other publications. Direct mail advertising campaigns to selected mailing lists featuring new product announcements and novel application stories --
2. Preparation of literature — product catalogs, specification sheets and application story bulletins --
3. Publications — internal company publications. External publications mailed periodically to selected customers. These may feature interesting application stories and technical articles. These articles may be written by customer personnel. Bulletins to the field organization such as a weekly or semi-monthly news sheet reporting company matters of interest including personnel changes --
4. Exhibits — preparation, construction and setting up product displays for national trade shows. Preparation and operation of mobile displays suitable for demonstrations to plant personnel. Design and preparation of portable demonstrators for use by the salesmen --
5. Mailing lists — building and maintaining customer mailing lists by market or product category. These are used in a variety of ways by all marketing and selling groups.

The advertising group reports to the chief marketing executive. It is considered a staff function despite the active, indirect selling role which it plays.

A well structured advertising group includes a group manager, editor, copywriter, technical writer, artist, exhibit manager, photographer and media buyer.

In small companies these functions may be handled by just a few people or some of them may be delegated entirely to the advertising agency that serves the company.

GROUP MANAGER

The Group Manager is well qualified in all aspects of advertising and sales promotion. This qualification results from extensive experience acquired in a company advertising group or by working in an advertising agency. He administers and has line responsibility for the group. He assists and advises in all functional areas. The most important contribution which he should make is to provide some of the imagination and creativity required to develop novel, hard-hitting advertising campaigns. He should also stimulate others to innovate and create in their particular specialties. He works closely with all of the specialists listed.

In the administrative area he assists in the development of the advertising appropriation and the departmental operating budget. It is his responsibility to evaluate the performance of his staff and the effectiveness of their work. He keeps informed, by association with related professional groups, of the development of new techniques and the emergence of new media and communication channels. He observes the productions of his competitors. He maintains close liaison with his superior and other staff members including the Product and Market Sales Managers and the Marketing Research group. He recommends and aids in the selection of the advertising agency, maintains close relationship and periodically evaluates its performance.

EDITOR

He is usually considered second in command, assists in some of his manager's duties and substitutes for him in his absence. He has the prime responsibility for formulating, outlining and editing the various productions including magazine advertisements and internal and external house organs. He supervises the selection and development of materials for catalogs, specification sheets, company publications and direct mail literature. He may assist in the preparation of technical articles for company publications and trade and technical journals.

COPYWRITER

He prepares materials for advertisements and direct-mail pieces, composes copy for these products, and he works with the art department in preparing layouts.

TECHNICAL WRITER

He prepares descriptive copy of technical subjects for the various publications, assists with other departments including engineering in the preparation of technical write-ups, and advises others in his group on problems involving technical subjects—this includes illustrations and photographic reproductions. He has responsibility for the technical accuracy of all material distributed outside the company.

ARTIST

The artist prepares art work in layout and finished form, coordinates and monitors art work purchased from the outside, and advises on type style and size, color schemes, and layout of copy.

EXHIBIT MANAGER

He plans product exhibits for trade shows and special purposes, designs and supervises construction of exhibits, arranges for trade show display space, and supervises the manning of exhibits by company personnel. The Exhibit Manager also plans mobile product displays, works with field sales manager and field supervisor in determining display itinerary, and supervises the driver-manager of mobile display.

He designs portable demonstration units for use by field salesmen.

PHOTOGRAPHER

He takes still and motion pictures of products, subjects for sales promotion, sales meetings and company personnel.

The photographer maintains a photographic darkroom, processes pictures and slides for various purposes, and keeps picture and slide files.

MEDIA BUYER

He assists in the selection of advertising media, handles negotiation of cost and space locations, reviews and checks agency schedules and media cost estimates, and maintains contact with media representatives.

This explanation of the advertising and sales promotion organization points out the many ways in which the group contributes to the selling and marketing performance. Too often this function may be looked upon as essential overhead and it may not receive its share of the credit for successful selling and marketing performance. With inspired leadership and the enthusiastic cooperation of all marketing groups it can do much to accelerate sales growth.

New Product and Market Planning and Development

Probably the most important corporate function in which the marketing department collaborates is planning for future growth. This does not mean the development of long-range sales projections and the techniques employed for them; it does encompass all considerations which can contribute to the growth in sales and profits for an extended future period—ranging from a minimum of three to a maximum of ten years. Unlike long-range sales projections, these considerations are not specifically concerned with economic factors. Most of the large progressive corporations have engaged in this function on a continuing basis in past years. Currently, it is very

PATTERN
FOR
GROWTH

popular, and many companies have recently initiated this activity or are contemplating doing so. The techniques employed are relatively new. They may differ in detail but the pattern of such planning is similar for the industrial equipment manufacturing industry which has been the prime concern of this book.

This planning function is being covered because it will give the salesman and his supervisors an appreciation of an important function which will influence their professional growth opportunities as well as those of the company. For the marketing staff, it may provide a basis for the initiation of new product and market planning and development efforts.

In the larger companies, this is a full-time responsibility of a member of the corporate staff. He provides the leadership and the initiative which is so essential to success. He may have a small supporting staff to aid in carrying out the many investigations involved. This manager usually reports directly to the corporate chief executive. The planning group manager is a member of the corporate

WHAT DIRECTION?

product committee. He may call on the sales and marketing chief and his staff for counsel and corroboration as needed. In small companies some semblance of this type of planning may be performed on an intermittent, part-time basis by the marketing department. It is an essential function for all companies — regardless of size — who are concerned about future growth and diversification. The outline which follows was developed under the direction of the author and was initiated by a typical, medium-size corporation with which he was associated. It reflects this company's particular circumstances just as all plans must. The circumstances which prompted the initiation of this function are quite typical, however.

The first step in initiating this function is to consider in what direction the company should expend its efforts. The determination of this direction involves the following preparatory steps:

1. The development of a list of proposed objectives--
2. A definition of new products--
3. A set of criteria for new products--
4. A product charter.

The following are examples of these steps:

1. Proposed objectives

   To pursue a policy of sound, profitable growth, to be achieved through proper balance between internal and external development.

   The company will maintain its position of leadership in its present product categories by continued adherence to high standards of product performance and aggressive marketing of these products.

   The company will seek to improve its current profits and return on investment through the addition of higher-return product areas, the elimination of unprofitable items, and by continuing cost-reduction efforts.

   The company will maintain an acceptable balance between government and industrial/commercial business. The government/military business should not exceed 50% in normal times.

   The company will diversify in the broad fields of measurement, control, test and recording, and communication and navigation equipment. Participation in these fields will be through components, instruments, equipment, and sub-systems.

2. A definition of new products

   A new product area is defined as a product or product line which requires a basic competency not now required for existing products. This competency may be new in one or more of the following functions: engineering, manufacturing, or marketing. Passive knowledge of, or past experience in, such a new product area does not constitute having the required competency. A new basic competency must be required for the primary function of the contemplated new product.

Product line extensions and maintenance are defined as updating, improving accuracy or performance, adding or changing features or dimensions or redesigning for cost reduction purposes. All of the foregoing would use the same basic technology used in the original product lines. Product line extension is further defined as involving the same basic engineering, manufacturing and marketing competencies.

3. A set of new product criteria
   A. Volume—A new product area should produce a minimum of one million dollars annual net sales after a reasonable introductory period. Generally this should be accomplished by the second full year of sales and shipments.
   B. Gross profit—The new product area should yield a gross profit, excluding development or other costs of acquiring, of at least 45%. If unusual marketing or other start-up costs are normal to the product, compensating adjustments should be made to this 45% target.
   C. Share of market—There should be a reasonable expectancy of reaching and maintaining not less than a 10% share of the market by the end of the second full year of active sales.
   D. Sales organization—The product line should be capable of efficient handling through the company's existing sales channels in the first year of active sales.
   E. Patents—Wherever possible, the new product area must have patent protection or other worthwhile proprietary protection.
   F. Technology—The new product must be of a highly technical nature in keeping with the traditional product lines. It should be of high quality, and should not be a type readily made by loft methods or other less technical operations.
   G. Payout—Amortization of development costs, tooling, capital investments and first year promotional expenses should be completed in two years. For an important acquisition involving plant, capital equipment and inventories, the payout should not exceed five years.
   H. Return—Pre-tax profit beyond the payout period must be 18% to 20% and the return on investment before taxes should approximate 30%.

For a variety of reasons, all new product recommendations may not meet each of the above requirements. However, they will be used as a set of standards against which to consider and measure new product activity before and after a new product is added to the line.

4. A product charter

This concerns the particular product interests of the company being used as an example and they, therefore, will not be included here. The charter is comprised of three sections.

The first section tabulates the product areas or broad categories in which the company's existing products fall. These areas are identified in generic terminology and not as specific product models. The purpose of this section is to provide a starting basis for future comparisons.

The second section of the charter comprises an initial list of recommended new product areas for consideration. They include suggestions from within the company as well as from outside sources. Although they represent considered opinions, they are not yet supported by thorough market investigation. This list is expressed in broad product categories or areas as in the preceding section.

The third section contains a comprehensive list of possible product lines. This extensive list is obtained from outside sources and the products may or may not fall within the realm of the company's present engineering and marketing capabilities. They usually have some market similarity, however. Some sources for these lists include government publications, product directories issued by trade publications and industry association directories.

PRELIMINARY SCREENING

Having completed these four preparatory tasks, the next step includes the identification of a number of these product area suggestions which appear to warrant more thorough investigation. This list of suspect areas is made up jointly by the product committee at the instigation of the planning manager. These are summarized in a form similar to that of the illustration. Each member including the chief marketing executive, reviews this summary and gives an indication of his interest--positive or negative. Supporting comments may be included. A positive interest indication signifies that in his opinion the product suggestion should be investigated further and that he would like more information.

A judgment is then made in selecting those suggestions from this summary for which there has been an indication of a broad positive interest. Some examples of forms used for this purpose are given in

```
┌─────────────────────────────────────────────────────────────┐
│                    PRODUCT PLANNING                           │
│                                                               │
│            SUMMARY OF PRODUCT SUGGESTIONS                     │
├──────────────────┬──────────────────┬────────────────────────┤
│ To               │ Location         │ Period covered         │
├──────────┬───────┴──────────────────┴──────────┬─────────────┤
│ Ref.     │            ITEM                      │  Interest   │
│ No.      │                                      ├──────┬──────┤
│          │                                      │ Pos. │ Neg. │
│          │                                      │      │      │
│          │                                      │      │      │
└──────────┴──────────────────────────────────────┴──────┴──────┘
```

For each item listed, check your interest 'Positive' (you want more information) or "Negative' (no interest). Comments are desired wherever possible.

Figures 78-80. Figure 78 covers some marketing criteria. These are rather elementary considerations. They can usually be evaluated readily. They are included primarily for the benefit of the other members of the product committee. The contributions of the marketing department to this screening function are much more extensive than these criteria. Figure 79 lists some typical criteria

PRODUCT PLANNING SCREENING		
MARKETING CRITERIA	RATING	REASON
Novelty of Product		
How urgent is the need		
What is the estimated market size		
Compatibility with present markets		
Will it diversify the company's markets		
Sales Growth - Possibilities		
Target selling price vs. Est. competitive price		
How will it influence customer and industry relationships		
Will it compete with large customers		
Qualifications of Sales Personnel		
Compatibility of sales organization		
Compatibility of advertising methods		
Compatibility of promotion methods		

Conclusions:

which apply to general management and to manufacturing and engineering management. Their purpose is to ascertain if present manufacturing and engineering facilities and talent are adequate for the proposed new product. Figure 80 covers some criteria which are more general in nature and some pertaining to financial considerations.

159

PRODUCT PLANNING SCREENING

CRITERIA	RATING	REASON
GENERAL		
Compatibility with corporate policy		
Contribution vs copy factor		
Protection possibility		
Possibility of establishing a foothold in a new technology		
MANUFACTURING		
Compatibility with manufacturing equipment		
Compatibility with building facilities		
Production know-how		
Compatibility with hourly line skills		
Compatibility with supervisory line skills		
Peace time raw material availability		
War time raw material availability		
Adaptable to mechanization & automation		
ENGINEERING		
Compatibility with engineering experience		
Availability of engineering equipment		
Availability of qualified engineering personnel		
Engineering content		
COMPETITION		
Number of competitors		
Strength against competition		
Strength against competitive R & D		

These rating procedures have been designed to help the product planning group and they are a necessary preliminary to an in-depth exploratory fact finding study. The screening guides are intended to encourage, not to limit the evaluation. The objective of these criteria is to generate thoughtful discussion of the proposed new product and not just a routine check listing. The decision arrived at, therefore, will be a judgment decision rather than a statistical one.

160

PRODUCT PLANNING SCREENING

CRITERIA	Check List		COMMENT
Facilitates the award of systems contracts		1	
Improves position to secure military contracts		2	
Offsets critical material and/or manpower shortages in event of war		3	
Improves position to serve and maintain contact with industrial and commercial markets in event of war		4	
Improves government, industrial, commercial sales balance		5	
Varies product line and minimizes effects of recession in any single industry segment		6	
Augments company recognition and prestige		7	
Dollar sales volume possibilities		8	
Profit possibilities		9	
Provides possibility of sales integration		10	
Provides possibility of advertising integration		11	
Offsets aggressive competition		12	
Permits manufacturing integration		13	
Secures tax advantages		14	
Permits sound investment of available assets		15	
Provides needed management, engineering, manufacturing and marketing personnel		16	
Provides needed plant and/or equipment		17	
Provides distribution system, sales force, etc.		18	
Provides patent rights		19	

(For extension of comments see reverse side)
Conclusions:

WHICH ROUTES

These screening steps and the selective fact finding investigations which follow covering the more promising new product possibilities result in a list of specific new product recommendations. The next

161

task is to consider which routes to follow to accomplish these recommendations. A number of routes may be taken. The most important ones include:

Internal Development
Acquisitions
Foreign Markets
Third Party Arrangements
Private Branding
Licensing
Joint Ventures
Outside Inventors

INTERNAL DEVELOPMENT

This is the route most commonly employed to obtain new products. It is an essential one to sustain and expand the company's present business. This approach is subjective in nature since its primary concern is with existing products and markets. Depending on the research and engineering capabilities present, it can provide a springboard to innovate related products which will diversify and expand the company's markets. Assuming the new product has been carefully checked in all aspects, it can be the safest and most closely controlled route to follow.

There are some hazards involved when small companies, who cannot do a thorough job of evaluating a truly new product, proceed with its development based on the enthusiasm of the engineering staff who envision a technical innovation or breakthrough. Such speculative development decisions usually result in R & D time and expenses well above the preliminary estimates. When the product is finally introduced, disillusions in the form of impenetrable competition or market saturation may appear which seriously limit the product's salability.

162

Innovations resulting from internal research and development often contribute patent rights which result in a strong competitive position and an assured, profitable sales growth. Internal development provides the best long range insurance for business stability. It is not the best route for realistic new product and market diversification goal achievement.

ACQUISITION

In recent years, this has been the most popular route to the accomplishment of new product and market objectives. There are various forms of acquisitions. The objective of some of them is to augment the company's present products with significantly different products which have good growth opportunity and are compatible with the company's market interests and its marketing organization and selling capability. This form is ideal for many situations but unfortunately such acquisition opportunities are not numerous and they may be difficult to find. Such opportunities do occur, however, and with a long range plan and a patient attitude, continued monitoring and search efforts may be rewarded.

Another popular approach is the conglomerate objective. Much of the recent acquisition activity falls into this category. Large corporations have expanded by acquiring, by various means, other substantial corporations whose product and market interests do not relate in any way to each other. The objective of the acquiring corporation is to increase its total sales and holdings rapidly without concern for compatibility of products or markets. This, then, has resulted in the formation of huge conglomerate corporations, most of which have experienced outstanding sales and profits performance.

There are several weaknesses in the conglomerate philosophy. One is that with widespread geographical locations and remote, decentralized management, the performance of the individual divisions tends to decline. Also, there is the constant threat of citation by the government for monopolistic restraint of trade under the federal anti-trust laws.

Factors favoring the first form of acquisition versus the internal development route are numerous. The acquisition route makes possible the achievement of the company's new product and market goals in the shortest time. Usually, if the acquisition prospect has been evaluated carefully, this is accomplished at a predetermined cost which is generally lower than the internal development route with its inherent new product failures as well as successes. Experienced personnel may be acquired who will broaden the company's areas of competence. The new products acquired in this manner are already known and accepted in the market place. Their profitability has been tested and proven by past experience. Usually they entail the least amount of risk. This is not assured, however, particularly where sophisticated, highly technical products are involved. It is more difficult to assess the future outlook for such products, particularly when they are in an area where the state-of-the-art is changing rapidly.

The procedures used in seeking acquisitions include:

1. Exploration and search to identify companies which could be desirable acquisitions--
2. Preliminary screening to pick out those which appear to match the established criteria most closely--
3. Investigation which involves assembling and studying all available facts. This may be done by reviewing company annual reports, product literature and other analytical reports. For those prospects who pass this investigation, a tentative proposal should be prepared, outlining the advantages to both parties of a merger and suggesting possible approaches which might be made--
4. Contact with company to ascertain the degree of mutual interest. This may lead to more complete investigation by both parties, utilizing each other's actual business records--
5. Negotiation involves the bargaining and other preliminaries leading to a legal agreement to acquire or merge--
6. The final phase is the consummation of the merger by forming an effective operating business combination.

FOREIGN MARKETS

Another desirable and well proven route is the exploitation of foreign markets. This has been done with marked success by many progressive companies since World War II. The European countries continue to experience sound economic growth and there is a sustained demand for sophisticated American-made products with advanced technical features. The technology in certain product categories has not caught up with the achievements of American manufacturers. This technical inferiority does not apply universally to all product areas in all countries. Some European countries are progressing rapidly in the sophisticated product areas. Most all have the technical competence but do not have comparable sources of low cost components which are available here.

Another possible advantage of foreign market exploitation is the exposure to foreign research and development. Many American companies have established research centers abroad, utilizing local engineering research talent to augment their efforts to seek and exploit new product ideas. This may result in completely new products or in licensing to utilize desirable patents. Cross-licensing, comprising an exchange of design data and patent rights is practiced commonly also.

164

A necessary consideration to facilitate sales abroad is to make provision for special export needs in designing products here, since standards such as electrical supply, wiring, and installation fittings are usually different. Provision for these variances can be made readily in the initial design stage.

To exploit foreign markets realistically requires a world-wide marketing approach. This can be done on a gradual basis concentrating initially on those countries which offer the largest present and potential markets. When these have been identified, the next step is to arrange for sales representation in those countries. Competent sales agents are available in all countries. One or more direct representatives are then located strategically, on a permanent basis, to select, train and support the sales agency personnel. When sufficient sales volume has been developed, the next step is to establish a branch factory and possibly a direct sales force utilizing local people. A carefully developed long-range plan, implemented on a gradual time schedule, can be an important contribution to the company's sales growth and diversification.

THIRD PARTY ARRANGEMENTS

The usual instigator of such an arrangement is a company which has a substantial, well-qualified selling and marketing organization and wants to increase its sales and profits by selling products made by others. There are many small industrial manufacturers of technically oriented products who cannot afford to have their own selling and marketing force. Their sales growth is limited accordingly and they may welcome the opportunity to expand their sales by utilizing the established selling and marketing organization of the instigator company. Obviously there must be compatibility of market interests of the two companies and of course their products cannot be currently or potentially competitive in nature. This may be an enduring relationship or it may be a trial period that can result in a merger or an acquisition. It is called "third party" because it comprises the manufacturing company, the selling and marketing company and the market which they jointly exploit. Sometimes this can lead to the formation of a joint venture.

PRIVATE BRANDING

This route has had limited application to engineered products of the capital goods companies. With some exceptions, it is utilized mainly by manufacturers of consumer products and appliances which are sold and marketed by large distributors and retailers. The large chain department stores are typical examples of this. An example of its application to the industrial products is when the product manufacturer sells to a non-competing manufacturer products which the latter needs, usually in limited quantities, to fill out his line or to

165

complete a system which comprises mainly products of his own manufacture.

LICENSING

Straight licensing consists of one manufacturer of proprietary products selling a permit to another manufacturer to make his proprietary products and to sell and distribute them using his - the licensee's - name. Such an arrangement usually involves an initial payment to cover engineering and manufacturing information and the right to manufacture them under the proprietor company's patents. Continuing payments are made in the form of royalties based on the number of products produced. This may be a quick and economical way to obtain a proven product line without the research and development costs and time.

JOINT VENTURES

This route closely resembles the third party arrangement, and is not used extensively. It has advantage when two manufacturing companies agree to work together in a joint venture to complement each other in the development and exploitation of a promising new market. One partner may have products which have markets which are radically different from the proposed new market area. The second partner may have products, which, in combination with those of the first company, could satisfy the new market requirements. The second company may also provide a selling and marketing organization which is qualified to exploit the combined product package. Neither company seeks to merge or to acquire the other. If the joint venture succeeds, a new separate company may be formed. Both companies would share the capitalization and ownership of the off-spring company.

OUTSIDE INVENTORS

Many companies use the talents of outside inventors to uncover new product ideas and designs. They serve to supplement the company's research staff and to provide new ideas. They may be useful also in providing an objective criticism of new products in their embryo stage and they may assist in evaluating acquisitions under consideration. Outside inventors are usually subsidized on a retainer basis. They invariably specialize in a technology which relates to the company's product interests.

This completes the description of eight of the available routes which may be followed to accomplish the company's new-product goals. Each route has some merit and the selection of one or more of them will be influenced by the size of the company and the specifics of its long range new product and market development objectives. They all complement each other. The policy of most corporations is to use all of them to the extent each makes sense to attain its specific objectives.

Progressive manufacturers cannot thrive without new products. In many successful companies, new products introduced in the past five to ten years contribute nearly half of their current sales. Predictions of the short-range outlook indicate that new products will contribute an increasing share of the nation's total sales, possibly comprising two-thirds or more. Companies can no longer rest on their past achievements and rely complacently on the continued impact on sales of products which were considered innovations ten or more years ago. The scientific and technological progress of nuclear techniques, oceanographic, space exploration, and many others has already created needs for equipment which were not envisioned just a few years ago.

All routes toward new products have some hazards. The majority of new products are failures. Most new product ideas do not get beyond the research phase. Others drop out in the development phase. Of those that survive these phases only about 50% achieve success in the market place. This means that to assure attainment of new product goals there must be some speculation and willingness to allow for this in the budgeting phase. Many ideas must be generated and tested since the percentage of success is low. This emphasizes the need to seek and test new product ideas continuously, utilizing several routes, to assure accomplishment of the company's growth objectives.

Wilbert H. Steinkamp

has devoted his entire professional career to selling, marketing and counseling others in the sale of complex, capital goods products and systems to industrial and government markets. Much of this experience has been acquired in the field where he served successively as a sales engineer, district and branch manager and national field sales manager, handling hundreds of sales engineers. For fifteen years he was a top marketing executive for three large industrial corporations where he recruited, trained, and supervised hundreds of sales and marketing people, both here and abroad.

In recent years he has worked independently as an industrial marketing consultant, counseling and assisting large companies in a wide variety of marketing and selling problems. He has created new professional training techniques. This book reflects in a logical, easily understood manner these many years of successful experience.

Throughout his career Mr. Steinkamp has taken an active part in pertinent professional organizations including the National Sales Executives Association, the American Management Association, the National Association of Manufacturers, the National Industrial Conference Board and numerous engineering societies and trade associations.